MW00365909

WHO'S LISTENING?

Other books by Jerry Johnston:

Why Suicide?
Going All the Way: The Real World of Teens and Sex
The Edge of Evil: The Rise of Satanism in North America
It's Killing Our Kids: Teenage Alcohol Abuse
  and Addiction
The Last Days of Planet Earth

Videos by Jerry Johnston:

Life Exposé
Why Suicide?
The Edge of Evil: The Rise of Satanism
It's Killing Our Kids: Teenage Alcohol Abuse
AIDS Among Teens
Are You Committed?
Kids and Gangs

To purchase any of these books and videos or to receive a catalog, write or call:

> Jerry Johnston Associates
> P.O. Box 12193
> Overland, KS 66282-2193
> (913) 492-2066
>
> Fax: (913) 492-3768

WHO'S LISTENING?

What Our Kids
Are Trying To Tell Us

JERRY JOHNSTON

ZondervanPublishingHouse
Grand Rapids, Michigan

A Division of HarperCollins*Publishers*

Who's Listening?
Copyright © 1992 by Jerry Johnston

Requests for information should be addressed to:
Zondervan Publishing House
Grand Rapids, Michigan 49530

Library of Congress Cataloging-in-Publication Data

Johnston, Jerry, 1959–
    Who's listening? : what our kids are trying to tell us / Jerry
Johnston.
        p. cm.
    ISBN 0-310-57870-1 (hardcover)
    1. Teenagers—United States. 2. Parent and teenager—
United States. 3. Teenagers—United States—Religious life.
I. Title.
HQ796.J5725   1992
305.23'5'0973–dc20   92-21865
                                                      CIP

Interior design by Bob Hudson
Edited by Lyn Cryderman

Printed in the United States of America

92 93 94 95 96 / ❖ DH / 10 9 8 7 6 5 4 3 2 1

To Al and Vidy Metsker—
Two people who loved and taught me like a son.
You have always had my respect.

Contents

Foreword

One of the great tragedies of our day is the widening gap between teenagers and their parents. We see it everywhere. Behind every teen pregnancy, every thirteen-year-old alcoholic, every suicide of a prom queen who seemed to have it made is a mom or dad who lost touch—a well-intentioned parent who quit listening.

In my years of working with young people, I can honestly say that most of the serious problems associated with teenagers could have been averted with properly expressed parental love. Most of the kids who went over the edge into sexual promiscuity, alcohol and substance abuse, or other aberrant behaviors could have been saved by a loving mom and dad who spent more time listening.

Who's Listening? is written by a dynamic Christian leader who really knows America's teenager, is a wake-up call to all of us, for if I were to answer the question raised by the title of this book, I would have to say that not very many of us are listening to our kids. We talk to them. We talk at them. We may even pray for them. But we aren't *listening*. And when a parent quits listening, believe me, our kids will find someone else who will listen. What's frightening is that there are lots of folks out there who are eager to listen to our kids: Folks like the producers of alcoholic beverages who "listen" to our kids through market research, then they package their product in ways that appeal primarily to teenage boys. Or the music industry, which "listens" to the raging hormones of post-adolescence and then delivers lyrics that link promis-cuous sex with violence and deviant behavior—people who have learned that by listening to a teenager they can discover how to mold and shape that person into what-ever they want him or her to be. They can peer into the hearts and minds of these young people and decode the valuable secrets so necessary for influencing them.

Jerry Johnston has spoken to more than 4,000,000 teenagers in high school assemblies across this continent. He has spoken one-on-one to thousands and has received letters and phone calls from thousands more. He has lis-tened to the sobs of a fourteen-year-old girl who has had an abortion and wants to kill herself. He has listened to the anger of a sixteen-year-old boy who lies paralyzed from a drunk-driving accident. He has listened to the con-fusion of a thirteen-year-old boy who thinks himself a homosexual.

Now, as *Who's Listening?* points out so clearly, it's time for others to start listening. Specifically, it's time for every mom and dad—every person in a position to influ-ence a teenager for the good—to start listening.

It sounds simple, but often the greatest solutions to the toughest problems are so simple that they evade us. We would like to believe that the answer is to improve our schools, provide more counseling, get the church more involved, or appoint another committee to study teen problems. Those things might help, but not until we start listening to our kids.

I hope that you let the letters in this book grip you as they have gripped me. I know from my own experience in working with teenagers that any one of these letters could have been written by a youngster who sits with his parents in church every Sunday morning. I also hope that

10

you pay close attention to Jerry's words of guidance and encouragement. If you do, we may be able to rescue a generation of young people who've given up on their parents' values. If we all start listening to our kids, we will hear the still small voice of our Lord reminding us, "Let these troubled children come to me."

Josh McDowell author of
How to Be a Hero to Your Kids

Acknowledgments

Credit belongs to Christie, my wife and best friend, who spent lengthy hours reading hundreds of letters from troubled teens. In the wee hours of the morning each letter reminded us anew of how important our work is to the youth of America. It is easy to lose sight of our contribution in the midst of the busy schedules, the draining travel, and the many days away from Christie and our children.

I would also like to say a word about my children: Danielle, Jeremy, and Jenilee. I once asked them if I should cut back on my constant travel and focus more on a career that would keep me at home. Their answers were unanimous: *No way!* They are the true heroes of this book. If I didn't have their support, I could not keep the heavy speaking schedule I maintain.

To all teenagers who have taken me into their confidence and shared what they may not have told anyone else, thank you. Your thoughts deserve our attention. It is my prayer that your letters will help parents try harder—to be more sensitive to and to communicate more effectively with their teens.

Introduction

It takes 150,000 dollars to raise a child from infancy to age eighteen according to a study commissioned by the Zero Population Growth Institute.

But it really takes more than money. Lots more. It takes the wisdom of Solomon, the patience of Job, the strength of Samson, the protection of a thousand guardian angels, and more love than most humans naturally possess.

I know, because I'm a parent, and I've spent the last ten years listening to your children. I've gone into more than 3000 schools across North America and spoken to nearly four million teenagers. I talk about life and love and sex and death and a lot of other things, and the kids seem to listen.

But I've been listening too. After every assembly, young persons gather around and start talking to me. After I leave, they write me letters. From listening to America's teenagers, I've learned some things that I almost wish I hadn't learned. I've learned that kids live in a world completely different from the world their parents lived in as teenagers. I've learned that pressure to use alcohol and other illegal drugs is almost impossible to stand up to—that girls almost the same age as my daughter have experienced group sex—that satanic rituals have attracted the attention of hundreds of young people—and that suicide has become an attractive option for far too many kids.

But far more urgent than all that, I've learned that teenagers feel as if no one cares about them—that no one is listening.

Initially I tried to convince myself that these teens were mistaken. "Your dad and/or mom really care," I would tell them. "You just need to talk with them." I might as well have been talking to a wall, for I could see in their eyes that my optimism wasn't shared. Over and over again the message came back to me: "My mom and dad don't care what I do, so why should I?" Or another favorite: "Every time I try to talk to my dad he just starts yelling at me."

The teens I talked to told me in no uncertain terms: "Our parents aren't listening to us."

So I decided to listen more carefully. Whenever I spoke at a high school, a flyer with my address on it was distributed to every teen. I couldn't believe the response. Thousands of letters have come in from kids from all across North America.

I decided to set up a nationwide hotline with a toll-free phone number for kids to call (1-800-SVA-TEEN), and the calls received from troubled teens now number into the thousands.

You wouldn't believe what they've been telling me. At first I didn't, either, but the neat thing about kids is that once they trust you, they really open up. They cut through all the pretensions that we adults expect from each other and get right to the heart of the matter. Believe me, it takes a little getting used to, but it's worth the effort.

I consider it a high honor to have so many teenagers writing and calling me. Now I want to share that honor with you. The crucial underpinnings of this book are the voices of America's teenagers. I've pulled together a sampling of the letters I've received, to let young people express the most urgent issues on their minds and in their hearts. My editors have trimmed the letters to conserve pages, and I've changed the names to protect the privacy of the senders, but none of the details have been changed.

I think that you'll see from these letters that America's teenagers have a great deal on their minds and need someone to talk to. But these aren't just "America's teenagers"—they very well may be *your* son or daughter. So I hope that this book will help you make the commitment to spend more time listening to your teenager.

Finally, I hope you will see that it really *is* possible to listen and talk with your teenager. All of us tend to preach to our kids. Doing so makes us feel good, but it doesn't work. In chapter 12 I have outlined my Twenty Prescriptions for Effective Communication, which will give you a better handle on really getting through with your teenager.

Raising your children through the teenage years is costly, but if you're willing to listen to them, it's worth the price tag. Don't give up on them . . . or on yourself.

1

SUICIDE

"I slit my wrists but not deep enough."

HI JERRY,

My name is Lucy and I was wondering how many pills you have to take to die. I want to kill myself but the only way I will is to take some sleeping pills. I want to kill myself because no one in my family wants me around and school is not going well for me and no one at school likes me. I'm so confused. Please help me.

LUCY

▼▼▼▼▼▼▼▼▼▼▼▼

19

DEAR JERRY,

My name is Donna and I will turn 13 next month. My life is a living hell. November 9 my best friend's brother shot himself in the head and died instantly. He was a freshman. Then this past October, Lisa hung herself in her closet. And just today my best friend writes me a letter telling me God is calling her to come and join her brother in heaven. I'm scared.

DONNA

▼▼▼▼▼▼▼▼▼▼▼▼▼

DEAR MR. JOHNSTON,

I've read your book over and over but I still can't find any reason to live. I almost killed myself tonight. I don't want to die but there's no other way out!

KIM

▼▼▼▼▼▼▼▼▼▼▼▼▼

JERRY,

By the time you get this letter I won't be alive. It's so hard to go on with the things I do daily. I supply all my friends with drugs. At home it's like being in hell already. My friends always think I'm happy but on the inside I'm burning up with hatred. To tell you the truth, my friend died because I started him on cocaine. Sometimes I want to cry to him and tell him I'm sorry. I just

BOB

▼▼▼▼▼▼▼▼▼▼▼▼▼

DEAR JERRY,

My name is Marci. I am a sophomore in high school. About two weeks ago my eleven year old brother tried to commit suicide. Can you tell me how an eleven year old could want to kill himself? There have been many suicide attempts in the elementary, middle, and high schools in the past month. And it's like no one gives a damn. The principals and superintendent feel it's just a phase we're going through.

MARCI

DEAR JERRY,

In October I was 15 years old and a sophomore in high school. My family situation was terrible, one problem after another. I got a plastic gallon milk jug and went out and filled it with gasoline. I poured it on myself. I lit one match and it went out but the second one didn't and before I knew it I was on fire. I was burned over 80% of my body and have 3rd degree burns except for my face. I lost part of my right leg last year because of a bone infection. I'm still here only by the grace of God.

BRIAN

DEAR JERRY,

Things have gotten much worse. I slit my wrists, but not deep enough. I was afraid. Not of dying but of the pain. I've been wearing short sleeves to supper for about a week now. You can see the scars plain, but no one has said anything about them to me. I guess that proves they don't care, don't you think?

AMBER

DEAR JERRY,

You really don't want to be around some low life satanist headbanger like me do you? What is it to you that a loner such as me thinks nothing but destructive thoughts. Thoughts of hurting others, mostly myself. Why should I continue to live in this uncaring world? My father beats the hell out of me; tells me how he hates me, how he wishes I was dead. Why not fulfill his wish? My 3.83 GPA means as much to him as the crap on the bottom of my shoe. No one cares what happens to me, a lost kid with no hope.

ADAM

▼▼▼▼▼▼▼▼▼▼▼▼▼

- Each year over 6,000 teenagers in the United States take their own lives.
- In 1950 suicide was the fifth cause of teenage death. By 1980, suicide accelerated to become the second greatest youth killer.
- Statistically, white teenage males commit suicide most frequently. Teenage females try more often, but do not always complete the act.
- Every 78 seconds a teenager attempts suicide. Every 90 minutes, one succeeds.
- Ten percent of teenage boys and 18% of teenage girls have attempted suicide.
- The suicide rate for Canadians under age twenty-nine has more than tripled in the past thirty years and is now nearly three times the national average of fourteen per 100,000 population.

▼▼▼▼▼▼▼▼▼▼▼▼▼

America's young today have a death wish unlike ever before. Although statistics regarding verifiable teenage suicides seem to have leveled off after the 278% increase from 1950–1980, plaguing questions still abound. Why are so many kids killing themselves?

Approximately 500,000 teens attempt suicide each year. Behind that actual gesture is an even more disturbing mind-set prevalent among youth: "Life is meaningless; why *not* kill myself?" Increasingly, the teens I talk with say that their parents don't care—that they never have time for them; that they never listen. Is it any wonder that suicide is never far from the minds of our kids?

One of the things I've learned as I've studied teen suicide is that kids are increasingly looking to more violent means to end their lives. According to the Morbidity and Mortality Report published by the Centers for Disease Control, there is an alarming trend among white females: They have become more violent in their efforts to kill themselves. Disappearing are the neatly lacerated wrists or the ingestion of sleeping pills. Guns reign as number-one, perhaps because they offer "insurance" that the job will be done right.

These violent efforts are hard to ignore. I have seen the carnage firsthand, and each memory is a nightmare. I will never forget seeing on the top of Peter's head, two eight-inch scars in the form of a giant "plus" sign. Peter had shoved a little pistol in his mouth. The bullet drilled its way through his head and lodged in the ceiling above him. In spite of our prayerful moment of silence on his behalf that night at an auditorium packed with 4000 kids, he died just a few days later.

I take little comfort in the accepted view that the rate of teen suicide has leveled off. The kids with whom I talk don't think that's the case. And my knowledge of the way that suicide is treated leads me to think that the numbers are still growing.

One suicide center in Minnesota believes that there are possibly 10,000 teen suicides per year, outnumbering deaths by accident. If this is accurate, suicide could be the number-one killer of youth. We know for certain that death certificate error and bias continue to abound nationally. Unless a note is found, many coroners will not term a death a suicide even if all other evidence points to such a conclusion. Yet, two-thirds of the kids who commit suicide never leave a note of explanation. Additionally, many automobile accidents involving a single teenage driver are disguised suicides. This much is certain: Too many kids are killing themselves.

Looking for answers

Just about everyone who works with young people struggles with the "Why" question. Why would a kid with a bright future ahead of him choose to end his life? Why would a girl from a family who regularly attends church swallow a bottle of sleeping pills one night? I wish I knew.

Some experts question whether today's young people have ever successfully bonded with their parents. Unlike previous generations, most kids today come from homes in which both parents are forced to work. No one's there when Sherry comes home from school after breaking up with Tom. No one's there to hear her pour out her sadness. No one's there to pat her on the back and tell her that it's going to be all right. A fairly typical and normal experience of youth looms as large and insurmountable: "If I can't have Tom, I don't want to go on living."

The disintegration of the American family is probably also a factor in the number of suicides. More than 12,000,000 kids live in single-parent homes with their unique set of challenges and problems. Divorce and remarriage often forces two sets of children to blend into one family, inevitably creating feelings of rejection, competition, and loneliness.

Have you listened carefully to music lyrics and paid attention to what's being portrayed in movies and television programs aimed at teens? Do so, to find another clue as to why suicide is popular. Frankly, I worry as much about the general theme of despair and hopelessness as I do about the outright references to suicide. A steady diet of heavy-metal music and slasher movies certainly contributes to a teen's suicidal feelings.

Finally, I have to lay a good share of the blame on drug usage. The "high" of a drug or drinking binge is always followed by the deepest of depressions. I know. Having been a young teen addicted to drugs, I know what it feels like to be seemingly living in a dark cloud. I wanted to kill myself. The echo of laughter from the last party seemed so distant. I couldn't even remember if I actually had had fun getting high.

Regardless of the reasons, if your son or daughter were the only person in the world contemplating suicide, you would still agree that suicide is a serious problem that demands our attention. Without being an alarmist, let me suggest that your son or daughter may *indeed* be dealing with thoughts of "ending it all."

So what can you do?

Help your teen to want to live

Put yourself in your teenager's shoes for a moment. Mentally walk the halls of his high school, where not wearing the right pair of shoes can result in cruel rejection. Where you're offered a joint from a sneering kid inside the doorway to the john—and if you turn it down, you'll be the target of derision. Where pressure is mounting to get good enough grades to get a scholarship to a good college. Where, perhaps, you just learned from the school nurse that you have a sexually-transmitted disease. Where the very walls of your life seem to be caving in on you.

I'm not one to glorify "the good old days," but my almost daily contact with high school kids convinces me that our children live in a very difficult world—one far different from the world of our own days in high school. They face more temptations than we did, and they face them earlier, often when they are emotionally unprepared to deal with them. How does a twelve-year-old deal with losing her virginity?

What your kids need from you to protect them from suicide is *empathy*. Understand their world and by all means take time to listen. We may know that there is absolutely nothing worth killing oneself over, but our kids don't know that. They desperately need you to listen to and hear their problems and then put them into proper perspective. They need to hear you say, "I know it must hurt to have been cut from the team, but maybe this will give you a chance to be in the school musical like you said you always wanted to try." They just need someone to show them that *all problems are temporary*.

As you listen to your teenager, you will be able to distinguish the offhand remark from the serious threat. It's not unusual for a teenager to say, "I wish I was dead." Don't ignore such comments but don't panic, either. If, however, you hear that comment more than occasionally and if you notice that your teen is becoming unusually despondent and prone to spending a lot of time alone, pay attention: Your teen may be crying for help. I recall one instance when a teen verbalized a death wish. His parent responded, "Don't let me ever hear you talk like that again." Big mistake. Be sensitive to your children. Read them daily like a book. Listen to their comments. Preventive concern and attention is far better than the trauma of a death, funeral, and final wishes at the cemetery.

Know the warning signs (see chapter 13). Don't delude yourself into thinking that only kids who abuse drugs and alcohol are the typical suicide victims. To a despondent teen any problem can seem too big to handle. Help your child through every crisis whether it be grades, dating issues, even little things like acne or a weight problem. Make their problems yours, and they will know that you care.

Also, don't live in denial, which is a form of pride. Humble yourself to face the fact that your son or daughter may indeed be considering suicide. Little problems turn into big ones that can breed destructive impulses. Identify with your son or daughter by understanding—not condemning—their hangups.

If you even half-suspect that your son or daughter is having suicidal thoughts, intervene with love and wisdom. Set up an appointment immediately with a qualified counselor. This single act shows your teen that you care. It is not overreacting! Talk with your school counselor, who in turn will notify your teen's teachers. Some schools even have a peer counseling program, pairing troubled teens with another teen who has had some basic training in listening skills.

This is also a good time to talk directly and candidly with your child. Ask him two questions: (1) You've been acting down lately, are you? (Identify with him: "I've been down too. In fact, there were times when I didn't think I could go on.") (2) Have you been thinking about a specific way to end your life?

I know that sounds abrupt and incredible. But those two questions must be asked when warning signs are exhibited. Believe me, your son or daughter will appreciate it even if at first he or she tries to brush you off. And if your teen was actually planning a suicide, your question will lead to prevention. If a teen has thought out a plan or method and has laid out a timetable, he is in immediate danger. Never leave him alone—and find qualified help immediately.

It has been said that suicide is really a frantic attempt to get attention. Are you paying enough attention to your teen? *You* can make a difference!

2

FAMILY PROBLEMS

"Our family used to be so close."

DEAR JERRY,

I hate my parents. All they ever do is nag and gripe at me. Especially my mother. Our family used to be so close, but me and my brother are constantly at each other's throats. He does things just to bother me. I hate him more than anybody in the world. On the outside my family looks so perfect and everyone envies me and my family. But if they were on the inside they would think differently.

SUMMER

▾▾▾▾▾▾▾▾▾▾▾▾▾

DEAR JERRY,

I don't know if I can hold on to what you call life but what I call a little taste of hell. I'm talking about what's happening with my family. My Mom and Dad had been drinking and they got into it and Dad hit Mom with a gin bottle. My brother was 11 and I was 8. Mom came screaming out of the room and we watched blood rush from her head and squirt onto the white walls and on my clothes and hands. Daddy left and I called the police and my aunt. Later Mom and Dad got back together but then split up for the last time. The final day of ever seeing Mommy and Daddy together was no get together. My brother and I were forced to choose who we were going to live with. Why did they do this to me Jerry?

KAY

▼▼▼▼▼▼▼▼▼▼▼▼▼

DEAR JERRY,

My parents are getting divorced and I wish that this was just a regular divorce. My father has gotten involved with a woman who has been married three times. Now I have all this hate—more hate than anyone can imagine. One day I'm going to blow up and do something. I need help.

NATALIE

▼▼▼▼▼▼▼▼▼▼▼▼▼

DEAR JERRY,

My parents separated and divorced in 1987. I was numb. I didn't talk about the divorce at all; I just tried to hide behind laughter and cute remarks. When my parents split, I had trouble deciding who to live with. I love both of them so much! I don't mean to be taking up so much of your time when I know there are many others who have worse problems. I

30

just felt that I needed to talk to someone and "spill my guts."

PAMELA

DEAR JERRY,

My mom has been married four times. I have nothing against her getting married, but she is going to have another baby. I've never really gotten along with my mom. We used to be close. But after she married her second husband and had my little brother and sister, and they got a divorce, it all changed. This man was strange. He did a lot of drugs. That's how I started to do drugs. My life is a total hell. I've already tried to kill myself twice.

DANA

JERRY,

I'm almost 16 years old and my parents are real strict. They won't let me do hardly anything. I mean they won't let me go nowhere with my girlfriends or date guys. And it makes me want to do it even more. I usually do but I feel guilty afterwards. I feel like I'm in prison with no key. Why are parents like that?

PENNY

JERRY,

Help! It seems everything is going wrong. I've done everything to try to get my parents attention. You will probably say talk to them. Well, all my dad does is yell! I don't want to live with my parents anymore.

I hate them! They are always too busy to pay any attention to me. Sometimes I think and believe my life is going down the tubes. Please help me.

CONNIE

▼▼▼▼▼▼▼▼▼▼▼▼▼

More than four million households representing mobs of kids are tuning in weekly to the Fox Television Network's mega-hit, "Beverly Hills 90210." Teen idols Luke Perry, Jason Priestly, and Shannon Doherty play students at West Beverly Hills High School in a series that has it all: AIDS, date rape, teen pregnancy, drunk-driving, death, and family problems. The show has captured America's attention.

What is it about this Aaron Spelling creation that jams malls with 4000 screaming teens when one of its stars makes an appearance? I'm afraid that part of its appeal is the simple fact that "Beverly Hills 90210" presents a picture of teen life that our young people recognize. One of the most alarming yet subtle features of the show is that virtually every family is dysfunctional: moms coked out; absentee dads; divorce; teens alienated from their parents. The kids we see are attempting to play a game called life, almost totally unassisted by their parents. With the exception of the Walshes—transplanted from an unhip outpost in Minnesota—family life on "Beverly Hills 90210" is anything but traditional.

It works because American teenagers know how close it is to the truth. The American family has broken down, and our kids are trying to pick up the pieces.

The modern American family

Much has been written about the demise of the American family, but what concerns me is what *kids* are telling me about their families. It's one thing to read the statistics about divorce, domestic violence, and other problems that make the Ozzie and Harriet family seem like a relic from some lost civilization on another planet. It's another to hear kids unleash their emotions about what goes on at home.

What are they saying?

They are frightened. Many teens are afraid that their parents may get a divorce. They hear them arguing at night over money or they see one parent flirting with someone at church, and they begin thinking that their family is about to disintegrate. Their fears may be unfounded—even healthy marriages experience disagreement and other stresses. But because so many of their friends have experienced divorce in their families, kids whose parents have *not* divorced are worried.

They are sad. I seldom see real joy in the eyes of the kids who talk to me about their home life. On the contrary, kids seem saddened about what's going on at home. Often I hear, "Both my mom and dad have to work so hard. I wish they weren't so tired all the time." Or, "We used to do a lot of things together, but now it seems as if we're all going our separate ways."

They are lonely. Because so many families are two-income families, kids are too often home alone—no one is home after school when a teen comes home needing to talk about something that happened during the school day. To compensate for their absence, many parents shower their kids with gadgets and toys. But Nintendo is no substitute for a heart-to-heart talk with Mom or Dad.

They are angry. Over and over again, children of divorce tell me how angry they are at their parents for splitting up the family. They don't like the every-other-weekend visit to Dad's place. They don't like having to begin calling a total stranger "Mom" or "Dad"—they don't like sharing a room with a new brother. Unfortunately, it's this pent-up anger that often leads to behavioral problems, thus placing even more stress on an already fragile family.

They are confused. Kids who hear preachers and politicians extol the virtues of family life then look at what's going on at home and wonder what they're missing. They want to enjoy coming home to a safe environment, but instead are too often nagged and berated for things that seem inconsequential. Can you imagine how a child must feel to be physically abused by someone he calls *Mom* or *Dad*?

Believe me, the kids whom I talk to in American high schools do not have many good things to say about family life.

Taking stock

I would be the last person to blame every parent for the problems our families are having today—being a parent is tough. I firmly believe that the traditional family is under attack. It's not all your fault if things aren't going as well with your family as you'd like. At the same time it might be helpful to take an honest look at your own family to see if there are things that you could be doing to give your teens a secure and loving haven from the difficult world of "Beverly Hills 90210."

There's no magic formula for taking stock of your family. It can be as simple as setting aside some time to talk with your spouse to make sure that you are both "on the same page" when it comes to expectations and discipline. Or you may benefit from a "town meeting" approach, where you gather the family together and ask all the members to identify two things they like about their family and two things that bug them. One of the things I hear kids say is that their parents don't listen to their complaints about siblings, rules, privileges, and the like. Wouldn't it be tragic if you thought that everything was fine with your family but that your teen hates coming home?

Every family has a tendency to mask its problems or ignore them, hoping that they will go away. But they won't disappear. In fact, ignoring them usually makes the problems worsen. In most cases, you may already suspect that your little "spats" and frequent bickering are more than the normal stresses of family life. Taking the time and effort to evaluate your family's state of affairs will help you identify the steps that you must take to get things back on an even keel. I can assure you that even the most awkward and clumsy attempt to heal your family's hurts will make a lasting and positive impression on your teenagers.

Hand in hand toward healing

The kids I listen to—America's high schoolers—want to go home to a healthy, happy family. That's what your kids want; that's what mine want. As a parent you have to take the initiative in repairing the damage to your family, even if the damage was not entirely your fault. For example, a belligerent teenager can work both parents against each other until a marriage is on the rocks. Two people who dearly love each other can actually separate because of the stress inherent in dealing with a strong-willed teen. I've seen it happen. If your family is characterized by fighting and tension, it would be easy to decide that it's not your fault and thus is out of your control. The right thing to do, however, is to commit yourself to working diligently toward restoring order to your family.

So let's start by looking at your marriage. Does your relationship with your spouse contribute to a sense of well-being in your family? Or have you drifted apart or become openly antagonistic toward each other? Most of the kids I talk with who have family problems point to a less-than-loving relationship between their parents. As the "core" of your family, you and your spouse help set the climate for everything that happens in your home. Therefore, take the necessary steps to put your marriage back in order. Don't be afraid to seek help from your pastor or a counselor. Too many couples wait until it's too late. Remember: You are not just saving a marriage. You are keeping a family together.

Try this little exercise with your teen. With your spouse, ask your teenager to comment on your marriage. You might be surprised. Teenagers have that amazing ability to cut through the pretense and give it to you straight. It could be that you thought that your marriage is a source of strength for your family, when in reality, your kids have noticed problems that bother them. By consulting with your teen, you are already beginning to reclaim a stronger sense of family and possibly opening the door for better communication with your teenager.

Of course, your marriage may be fine, but you still find yourself and your spouse arguing with your teenager more than usual. Simple conversations quickly escalate into full-fledged battles so that you all go out of your way to avoid talking. Don't be *too* hard on yourselves, because part of growing from adolescent to adult involves challenging one's parents. It happens and is quite normal. It becomes a problem, however, if most of your interaction is negative. What do you do when the gulf between you and your teen widens to an uncomfortable (and unhealthy) level? Consider the following options:

Face the problem head-on. Don't wait one more day to address the situation. Get things started *now* by picking your son or daughter up from school, stopping for a malt, and saying, "Hey daughter of mine, I love you, but it seems like none of us are getting along as we should. Let's try to change that." Don't try to solve everything over that one malt. Just extend the olive branch and try

36

to leave the place with everyone wanting "things" to go smoother.

Lead with your life. So many kids tell me that "My mom says one thing and does another." Or, "He wants me to do things *he* won't even do." If you insist that your daughter speak more respectfully to her mother, you had better make sure that *you* speak to your wife more respectfully. And by all means, if you've been unfair to your teen or unkind to your wife, apologize. Watch your speech.

Lighten up. If you want your teen to enjoy his family, make it fun to be part of your family. And don't *look* for trouble. Ignore the little things and don't throw a fit over the big things. Dads, when was the last time you wrestled on the living room floor with your son? Moms, wouldn't it be fun to spend an evening trying new hairstyles and experimenting with makeup with your daughter? Ask yourself this question: If I were a teenager, would *I* want to come home and spend time with me?

Be direct. If you sense that something may be wrong with your teen, don't try to tiptoe around the problem. Kids appreciate honesty. Without accusing or insinuating, ask straightforward questions: "Are you having sex?" "Is someone trying to take advantage of you?" "Did I embarrass you?" If you get an answer you don't want ("Yes, Tim and I made love last night"), don't blow up. It's one thing to express disappointment—even to discipline—but you will accomplish nothing by becoming angry when your teen gives you an honest answer.

Don't legislate spirituality. Too many kids from Christian homes leave the faith because their parents tried to force them to believe. By the time a child is sixteen, she may raise questions about the spiritual truths that she has been taught. Personally, I think this is great because it gives us a tremendous opportunity to talk about faith. But many parents become alarmed and respond with ultimatums such as, "I don't ever want to hear you ask such a ridiculous question again." As a parent you need to insist on a reasonable level of involvement in church activities, but beyond that your teen needs to be given room and freedom to decide on the key issues of Christian faith.

Seek help. If your efforts to get your family back on an even keel don't seem to be working, take advantage of the numerous, excellent, family resources that are in most communities. Check with your pastor for the names of reputable family counselors. Often a school social worker can mediate disputes between you and your teen. I've found that sharing concerns with a Bible study group or Sunday school class can be extremely helpful. When you go to the "trouble" of finding professional help, you are telling your family that "We are important enough to warrant special attention."

Today's alienated teenagers yearn for the closeness and support that comes from a healthy family. Mom and Dad: Is your family important enough for you to take steps toward repairing your marriage relationship? Do you need to take the initiative with your kids in tackling some of the things that are pulling your family apart? How I'd love to visit the high school in your town and have your child come up to me afterward and say, "Jerry, I'm really lucky. Our family's pretty cool!"

3

VIOLENCE

"I'm in jail for murder."

MR. JOHNSTON,

> I hate my stepdad more than anyone in the whole world. He tries to rule my life. He keeps me grounded all the time. I've told him I hated him and you know what? He grounded me. I can't figure out if it is his way to split him and my mom up. I don't try, but I wish they would. One time they almost got divorced and I wasn't a bit sad. I was overjoyed until they made up and once again I got blamed for it and grounded. Getting grounded is one thing, getting back at me is another. I think if I killed anyone right now without regretting a moment of it, it would be my stepdad. If someone doesn't help me or give me logical advice I will take his life.
>
> COLETTE

▼▼▼▼▼▼▼▼▼▼▼▼▼▼

DEAR JERRY,

I am in jail for murder. I was on drugs the night this so-called friend got me in this mess. I was with them when they cut this girl's throat and stabbed her in the head twice and once in the back and cut her from her throat down below her breast. I was scared to death. She looked up at me and begged me to put her out of her misery. I didn't know what to do. They told me to do it so I stabbed her one time. I gave myself up to the law and now I'm going to court to try and get them.

HAL

▼▼▼▼▼▼▼▼▼▼▼▼▼

DEAR MR. JOHNSTON,

I am 15 years old and I'm writing to ask your help in solving a problem. Today a girl on the bus pulled a 10-inch long knife on me. I told the principal and he asked whether I wanted to press charges. I thought about it all day and decided it would be best for her if I did. Maybe she will get the help she needs. All day she said after she killed me she was going to kill herself. That was all she talked about. I really feel the teachers in this school do not believe that some-thing like this would happen in our school.

MARTIN

▼▼▼▼▼▼▼▼▼▼▼▼▼

DEAR JERRY,

My life became a living hell in the seventh grade when I started hanging out with the wrong people because no one else would accept me. When I started hanging around the stoners I thought I was cool. I started taking speed and crack. I dropped out of the eighth grade and my drug problem wasn't making my home life any better. I started cruising the streets and going to parties. I started taking cocaine and that only got me into more trouble. I ended up getting arrested and put in juvenile hall because I beat up my mother. I thought that first time in jail would straighten me up. As it is I've been arrested more than ten times and in and out of jail seventeen times.

MEGAN

▼▼▼▼▼▼▼▼▼▼▼▼▼▼▼

DEAR JERRY,

My name is Scarlet. I am in a psychiatric hospital for drugs, alcohol, family problems, and physical aggression to my mother and stepfather. I have been here for over a year. I haven't gotten anywhere. I feel useless and no good. I'm really feeling down. What should I do?

SCARLET

▼▼▼▼▼▼▼▼▼▼▼▼▼▼▼

Are these really our kids? Can these possibly be the fresh-faced youngsters whom we watched as they played in the backyard ten years ago? How did they learn to kill? Where did they get all this aggression?

We hear talk about our school grounds becoming battlegrounds, and I can assure you that it's true. Between 1986 and 1990, sixty-five students and six school employees were killed with guns in schools; 201 were severely wounded; 242 people were held hostage. An estimated 3,000,000 crimes occur each year on school grounds. One study estimates that on a typical day 100,000 pupils carry guns to school. And in a recent highly publicized study conducted by the Center for the Study of Social Policy, violent-death rates for kids age

41

fifteen to nineteen have jumped by 11% during the last decade.

One school district in a major city proposed to install metal detectors at the entrances of the public schools. Estimated cost: nine million dollars. A frivolous expense? Hardly. School administrators revealed that there were almost 2000 incidents of students carrying firearms and an additional 1,270 assaults in that district.

Gangs have become the surrogate family of the 1990s. The United States Justice Department estimates that there are between 125,000 and 250,000 gang members across the country. Count the kids who are vying to get into the gangs, reports the Justice Department, and that number goes up threefold. And we're not talking only about Los Angeles and New York. Malcolm Klein, director of the Center for Research on Crime and Social Control at the University of Southern California, says that there are a known one hundred twenty-six U.S. cities in which gangs have been established.

Violence among youth is increasing. According to a Justice Department report, teenagers are much more likely than adults to be victims of crimes of violence. On the average, there are sixty-seven violent crimes per 1000 teenagers each year, compared to only twenty-six per 1000 adults age twenty and older. About half of all violent crimes against teens occurred in school buildings, on school property, or in the street.

For black young people the problem of violence is especially severe. Of black males in the U.S., one in twenty-one dies of murder. Homicide is the leading cause of death for black young men. They are three times more at risk to be murdered than white adolescents.

Why so violent?

When I read statistics that document the rise in violence among young people, I am dumbfounded. How

42

could a person who has lived only thirteen to nineteen years become so violent? Why do our kids opt more and more for aggression? Although I do not have many answers, I have some hunches. Certainly television is one of the primary factors in the growth of violence among youth. I know that TV can become a favorite scapegoat for just about every problem in society, but consider how many violent images your children see when they watch television: The National Coalition on Television Violence reports that by the age of eighteen, a child will have seen 200,000 violent acts on television, including 40,000 murders!

Read that last sentence over again, and then think about it the next time you read in your local newspaper about a teenager who has shot someone. Would reaching for a gun seem as natural had that teen never seen so many graphic, slow motion scenes of someone shooting another person on television?

If you haven't already seen for yourself, try watching one of the action-packed dramas on prime-time television. Invariably, you will see scenes of violence that were unthinkable twenty years ago *in the movies!* How might it have affected you if, at the tender age of ten or eleven you saw a rape scene graphically acted out on television? How might you have responded to an insult in the lunch line at school if you had seen numerous assaults on television while you were in your formative years? Television is certainly not the only reason for an ever increasingly violent generation of teenagers, but it must accept some of the blame.

I am convinced that the rising number of fractured families is also contributing to teen violence. Elementary school teachers will tell you that they can easily detect when a student's parents are experiencing marital problems. It almost always manifests itself—especially in boys—in aggressive behavior at school. Psychologists explain that a child's anger caused by what's happening between Mom and Dad explodes on the school playground or in the classroom. Without someone to talk to about those problems, kids bottle it up until the rage can no longer be contained.

Drugs are an obvious factor in teen violence. First, some drugs like speed and crack stimulate the nervous system to the point where a young person is "on the edge." Even the smallest affront or inconvenience can push him over the edge. Drugs are more likely to lead to violence, though, in turf battles and rivalries between competing dealers. Many kids have to sell drugs to afford buying them, thereby increasing the likelihood of offending another dealer.

Tragically, child abuse often results in the victim's becoming violent as he or she becomes a teenager, and the constant barrage of violent images and thoughts in rock music, comic books, video games, and movies must also surely account for a generation of violent teens.

But there's one other factor, one that might hit closer to home: mistaking "macho" for masculinity. Obviously this relates solely to young men, but for some reason we have elevated the notion of being macho to a near godlike status. Movie heroes are guys with big muscles, big guns, and big egos. The male athlete is almost worshiped, while the scholar is often the butt of cruel jokes. The trend in stand-up comedy is to follow in the footsteps of the late Sam Kinnison who raged on stage against women and got big laughs. Fraternity hazings (and their dormitory counterparts on Christian college campuses) send a message that it's perfectly acceptable to gang up on another individual, the justification being that "boys will be boys"—it's a manly kind of thing. That's the rationale, but I don't buy it, and neither should you.

Escape from the killing playgrounds

It's important that you know the kind of battlefield our teens walk through every day as they attempt to get an education. As I talk with teens about this, I sense a high degree of fear and anxiety (which can prompt even the most timid teen to strike back in violent anger). Often our kids are afraid to go to school, but they don't want to admit it.

I recall talking with a colleague who told me of going to tuck his teenager into bed, something he hadn't done since the boy was a youngster. For some reason, he decided to step into the bedroom, pat the boy on the back, and just say goodnight. His son, however, appeared agitated about something, so my friend wisely initiated some small talk. Within a few minutes his son blurted out, "Dad, you have no idea what it's like to go to my school. I'm scared to death half the time!" Deep sobs followed as father and teenage son held each other.

This dad was fortunate. There are countless other moms and dads who first learned about their teenager's violent world when their son or daughter was assaulted. Many kids who would never think of hurting anyone are carrying knives to school, just in case they need it for self-defense. One of the reasons that so many kids are joining gangs is that the gang is seen as a source of protection. Better to join and have someone on your side when the fighting starts than to go it alone. Although teens in urban and suburban schools are more likely to encounter violence than are their rural counterparts, the heartland is also experiencing an increase in violence among young people.

As parents we all have an obligation to protect our kids. Most of us feel adequate to the challenge as long as our kids are with us, but what about the six to eight hours a day they are in school? What do we tell a fifteen-year-old who tries to sneak a knife in his book bag in order to protect himself from the group of guys who are out to get him? What do we tell a daughter who's afraid to walk home from the bus stop?

The familiar rules of self-defense ought to be impressed upon every teenager: Travel in groups or at least with another friend; avoid darkened stairways, cul-de-sacs, and vacant lots; make sure that someone else knows where you are; stay away from drugs and locations where drugs are used or sold; if a fight breaks out, don't gather around to watch; and don't wear expensive jewelry or carry large sums of money.

Make sure that your teen knows the importance of reporting any harassment or threats to school officials and parents. If the behavior continues, she should contact the police (or have her parents do it) as well as the school. This isn't 1950, when the school bully talked tough and occasionally started something that ended up with two guys wrestling on the ground for a few seconds until a teacher broke it up. Today's fights at school often involve knives, baseball bats, and guns. Take your teen's fears seriously.

In my work in America's public schools I have found high school principals to be vitally concerned about the safety of their students. They will do their best to address your concerns and respond to your requests. However, if your teen is being constantly accosted and you feel that the school is not doing enough to prevent such behavior, it might be necessary to request a transfer to another school in the district. Or you might consider keeping your teen home from school until you get a satisfactory response. If you take this step, though, make sure that you let the school know what you are doing and be ready to follow through if they propose a solution. I usually do not recommend such drastic steps, but if your child's safety is in jeopardy, dealing with a truant officer will be better than coping with a serious injury.

Quieting the rage

Just as it is important to protect your teen from the violence of others, you may also need to protect your son or daughter from the rage *within*. Remember, your child has grown up in a world of violent images. Raging hormones, peer pressure, and fear can combine to provoke even the most mild-mannered teen to uncharacteristic violence. There are times when I have almost felt the tension in high school hallways and classrooms, and so I'm not surprised when I hear about a tragic outburst of violence in our high schools. What's surprising is that some of these incidents involve kids who have not been much of a problem in school.

You can go a long way to help quiet the rage within your teen by making sure that he or she has some daily quiet time and privacy. By "quiet time" I especially mean time without the stereo or television as background noise. Your teen needs a break from the driving, frenetic pace of so much popular music (even Christian contemporary music). Try to impose a "noise-free" time for everyone in the house, guaranteeing at least a few minutes of silence each day. If you can encourage your teen to spend some of this time in prayer, thinking about God, or reading the Bible, you will be that much more ahead of the game. Please don't make this time seem like a punishment but make it more of a reward ("You deserve some peace and quiet").

I know it's not always possible to provide a private bedroom for every child, but during the teen years privacy becomes extremely important. If you cannot give your teen her own bedroom, try to find a place in the house (a study or den) that could be "reserved" for her regularly. And respect your teen's privacy. Knock before entering. Never barge into the bathroom when your teen is using it. Don't pry too deeply into your young person's thoughts. I've had some teens tell me their parents always seem to be intruding into their lives. That may be an overstatement on their part, but sometimes we forget that they need time with their thoughts just as we do.

Make sure that your teen has a trusted adult to talk to when pressure and confusion mount. A teen needs to be able to blow off a little verbal steam now and then or the explosion will be physical. Don't assume that your teen knows whom to go to. School counselors are always available, but most high school students view their counselor as someone who's there to give them advice about their class schedule and college. You may need to suggest some people (i.e., teachers, a coach, a youth pastor) who would be willing to be a confidant to your teen. Sometimes just knowing that someone is available is enough to quiet the heart of an anxious teen.

My friends in the health and wellness movement stress the importance of exercise, nutrition, and adequate rest in combating the kind of anxiety and stress that can result in violence. I sometimes wonder if they have ever tried getting a teenager to eat sensibly and get enough sleep, even when their advice is sound. A bowl of sugared cereal and a pastry in the morning sends your teen off to school virtually wired for action. Avoid it. Do your best to encourage some type of *fun* physical activity (biking, touch football games, tennis, etcetera). Better yet, do some of these activities *with* your teen. It's amazing how whacking a tennis ball or kicking a soccer ball can release frustration.

We are all painfully aware of how much we teach by example, and the way that we handle our own anger certainly speaks volumes to our kids. Slamming doors, doing a "slow burn," losing control, yelling, and so forth, are the kinds of behaviors that no adult is proud of, but when our kids see us do these things regularly it becomes part of their repertoire for responding to anger. If you tend to lose control often, admit it to your teen and acknowledge that it is wrong. That kind of honesty will generate a tremendous amount of respect for you as well as communicate the message that such behavior is wrong.

The whole question of television, movies, and objectionable music needs an entire book to deal with adequately. I recognize that different families have different standards, so it is difficult to generalize on these issues. Personally I believe that the graphic violence portrayed in these media are potentially harmful to teens and subtly encourages them to be inclined toward violence when under stress. But I also know how difficult it is to monitor everything our children see or hear. A thirteen-year-old girl once said, "Hey, my own *life* is R-rated, so why shouldn't I be able to go see an R-rated movie." Regardless of your own family's standards on these media, I highly recommend discussion of violence in the media with your teen. Talk about it. Express your concerns about how such images and ideas settle into the dark recesses of our minds. Then *listen*.

4

HOMOSEXUALITY

"I battled it for years until I caved in."

DEAR JERRY,

As much as I hate it, the truth is I'm a homosexual. If this turns your stomach believe me, it's even worse than you think. No sin could be worse than this sin. It consumes a person like cancer. It controls me. It is on the verge of destroying me. How do I get rid of this perversion? Can I ever marry a woman and look her in the eye? Nothing could be worse than the guilt and dirtiness I feel.

KEVIN

▾▾▾▾▾▾▾▾▾▾▾▾▾▾▾

DEAR JERRY,

I'm gay. I can't live with it because it goes against everything I believe in. I already know that I'm too much of a coward to shoot myself so I've decided to get real drunk and have an "accident." I've decided that when I kill myself I'm going straight to hell. I'm tired of being lonely. I'm writing to you because I have no one else to tell my story to.

RANDY

DEAR JERRY,

At 15 I was sexually assaulted by my gym teacher. I was afraid to tell on him. I started being a prostitute on weekends. I would leave school on Friday, go downtown, and return home Sunday nights. I had money and drugs and booze. All I needed. James was 19. I was his first love. Every time he left I tried suicide.

JAY

DEAR JERRY,

About three years ago I started masturbating. It's gotten to where it's an obsession. Sometimes I fantasize about girls. While all my friends are talking about the finest guy in school, I'm thinking about who the finest girl is. I want to be normal.

NANCY

JERRY,

I am a 17-year-old male. I am now sitting in an adolescent psychiatric unit after my sixth suicide attempt (four since becoming a Christian). I struggle with issues of homosexuality and sexual addiction. My dad is an alcoholic and well—the dysfunctional family just like every other American teenager. I'm not suicidal now, but I'm afraid of the depression that can come over me at anytime.

STEVEN

▼▼▼▼▼▼▼▼▼▼▼▼▼

JERRY,

My problem is that I'm a homosexual. I have been this way ever since I can remember. My doctor told me that it is genetic and that nothing I do will change me. I never chose to be this way! I hate myself because I am like this. I have asked for God's help but my desire did not cease.

RYAN

▼▼▼▼▼▼▼▼▼▼▼▼▼

DEAR JERRY,

I am a homosexual. I battled it for years until I caved in. I've read all the Scriptures on the subject and pondered them. Although I can't say that I know precisely what Romans 1 is saying on the matter, it is frightening.

SAM

MR. JOHNSTON,

I'm 14-years-old and I'm bisexual. I am also having sex with my brother because he wanted me to. Eight months ago I tried to cut my life short by swallowing 280 pills. I need your help.

CARRIE

▼▾▼▾▼▾▼▾▼▾▼▾▼▾

Daniel Paul Layer was one of several young people featured in *Newsweek* magazine's fall 1990 special edition on teenagers. His story appeared in the startling section, "Coming Out Now." It described his odyssey of being gay and unashamed. His mother is supportive, and his homosexual lifestyle is reinforced by group therapy sessions with other gay teens. He is determined to settle down with a man, adopt three children, and live a happy life.

I have met many young men like Daniel. They are in every high school in North America. They are often polite, well mannered, and good students. As I have traveled across the country and visited schools, I have noticed the emergence of the gay lifestyle among youth. It is, I am convinced, one of the major trends among teens today. I predict that by the end of this decade the cultural bias against a homosexual lifestyle will be eliminated in the public school sector. It will be common to see gay couples on the high school campus "uncloseted" and unconcerned. And those who raise objections to this lifestyle will be scorned by gays and straights alike.

The message from the media

How could this happen? Why has it suddenly become almost fashionable to be gay? What could lead a Christian teenager to say, "It doesn't matter really whether you're gay or straight, as long as you have an honest and loving relationship"?

A quick spin of your TV dial and opening your eyes to the messages beamed from the silver screen will give you a clue. The popular television show, "L.A. Law," featured an episode showing an intimate kiss between two females. The *Dynasty* miniseries reunion enunciated Steven Carington's overt homosexual relationship that had been previously expressed and dramatically reinforced. Numerous actors and actresses have played homosexual characters: William Hurt in *Kiss of the Spider Woman* (for which he won an Oscar); Cher in *Silkwood* (Oscar nomination); Robert Redford in *Inside Daisy Clover*; Meryl Streep in *Manhattan*; Harry Hamlin in *Making Love*. *The Butcher's Wife*, starring Demi Moore, presents the joy of one troubled New York career woman who finally achieves satisfaction through a lesbian relationship.

Is it any wonder that many of the mobs of young people who view these films and television shows begin to question their own sexuality? Strengthening the gay cause are youth icons like Madonna who has openly confessed to being bisexual. Her "Truth or Dare" rockumentary poises her as a "mother" to her homosexual dancers, shows her performing fellatio on a bottle, and showcases other gender-bending scenes. Did you notice how many winners at last spring's Oscars thanked their "life partner"? They weren't talking about a business partner, were they? Every time another musician or media hero comes out of the closet, a teenager's resolve to believe in the biblical model of sexuality that you taught him is weakened. He's already at the age where rebellion and the questioning of his parents' values is normal. Maybe homosexuality is normal, too, he thinks.

If your son or daughter desires to taste the forbidden fruit of a gay lifestyle, opportunities abound. The homosexual agenda is all-inclusive with its publishing companies, gay bars, clubs, magazines, political lobby, and much more. It is a movement highly interested in recruiting new members, and what better recruit than a confused and rebellious teenager?

I do not want to sound like an alarmist, but I do want you to comprehend the kind of world that your son or daughter is experiencing. When you were young, a homosexual was queer, not gay, and he tried to hide his homosexuality because it was dishonorable to be homosexual. Consequently, you had no desire to experiment with homosexuality. That simply is not the case today, and the teenager knows this better than you do.

Why you should care

Just for the sake of argument, let's assume that although you believe that homosexuality is forbidden by Scripture, you have decided that your son or daughter should have the freedom to choose his or her sexual orientation. It's a line I'm hearing often these days. But a live-and-let-live attitude just doesn't work when it comes to homosexual lifestyles because the effects of a homosexual lifestyle are being understood as increasingly dangerous. First, the risk of AIDS is higher for those who engage in unprotected sex with homosexuals than it is with heterosexuals. Second, the incidence of suicide is higher among homosexuals than among heterosexuals.

Let me make one point clear from the beginning: I realize that AIDS is not a "homosexual disease" but a disease that is spread primarily through sexual activity and intravenous drug use. Period. Although the homosexual community seems to suffer more disproportionately than does the heterosexual community, the disease can strike anyone. And I also recognize that in rare instances a person can get AIDS from "innocent" activity such as a blood transfusion (as the recent tragedy of Arthur Ashe has demonstrated). Further, I support efforts to accelerate the research toward finding a cure or more successful treatment.

But we are doing a disservice to our teens if we do not warn them of the dangers of AIDS and explain that they may be more likely to encounter it in a homosexual lifestyle than in a heterosexual one. And whether we are talking about homosexuals or heterosexuals, I do not believe that we should simply encourage the use of a condom or other forms of "safe sex." *We need to teach our kids the value of celibacy before marriage, of forming proper and chaste relationships, and of postponing sexual intercourse until marriage.*

When they link AIDS to homosexual lifestyles, Christians are often accused of "bashing" homosexuals, but it's the homosexual community that seems to be guilty of slanting the truth. In a very deliberate and organized campaign the gay community has tried to eliminate bias in the language of AIDS.

Instead of identifying "risk groups" that would include homosexuals, the politically correct term is "risk behaviors." Instead of the term "homosexual sex," we are encouraged to refer to "anal intercourse," presumably to include heterosexuals and not call attention to a popular sex act with male homosexuals. The homosexual lobby objects to the term "innocent victim" to describe someone who contracts the disease through a blood transfusion or unsanitary medical procedures. Why? It implies that homosexuals are guilty.

All of this conditions teens to think of homosexual behavior as innocent and legitimate. They rightly learn that AIDS is not necessarily a disease restricted to homosexuality, but their objections to homosexual lifestyle also become softened. Thus, protection becomes the only virtue in sexuality. It matters little if you are homosexual or heterosexual—Wear a condom and be true to your partner! becomes the rallying cry.

Knowing that AIDS is rampant in the homosexual community and that even the wearing of a condom is not a foolproof protection from the disease, do you really think it's okay for your son or daughter to experiment with sexual orientation?

Beyond the threat of AIDS there is an even more subtle danger involved in the homosexual lifestyle, especially as it relates to teens. Paul Gibson, a San Francisco social worker who conducted a study of youth suicide for the U.S. Department of Health and Human Services, believes that gays account for 30% of all teen suicide attempts. Furthermore, the department's Secretary's Task Force on Youth Suicide reveals that gay and lesbian youth are two to three times more likely to attempt suicide than are other young people. As many as 30% of all teen suicides may have been related to sexual identity issues.

The Journal of Counseling and Development reported on a study of 1000 adult homosexuals that found a higher rate of suicidal thoughts among homosexuals than among heterosexuals. Of those who had considered suicide, more than one-half of the men and one-third of the women implicated sexual orientation "as a precipitant."

To young teenagers infatuated with the unisex and gender-confused images romanticized by rock groups and contemporary fashion, a little walk on the wild side of the homosexual lifestyle may seem appealing. But if they know the facts—if we do our job of educating them about the hazards associated with homosexual lifestyle—I'm convinced that we can save our teens from falling into the promiscuous and desperate world of homosexual sex.

A few months ago I visited the phone banks of the nationwide AIDS hotline (800-234-TEEN). It was a sobering experience. Do you realize that in 1991 this hotline for kids who worry about AIDS received 26,000 calls?

They were calling to ask about safe sexual practices, many expressing their fear that they have the virus. Astounding to me is that every call is answered by another teen. Some are straight, some are gay. Think of it! Teenagers seeking advice on one of the deadliest diseases around, getting their information from someone their age who may or may not be gay. Does that strike you as being an anomaly?

I have since learned that kids are more likely to get their information about sex from other kids than from adults or trained sexual counselors. In a recent survey of teens, 52% listed their friends as their primary source of information on sex- and health-related issues, while only 10% listed their parents as their main source of information on the subject.

Keeping your child straight

I hold strongly to the view that homosexuality is learned behavior or the result of influential factors such as a dominant mother, a distant father, or child abuse. Therefore, I believe that it is possible to prevent most children from becoming homosexuals. The best place to start is in your own marriage. Your children ought to see the virtues of a heterosexual relationship by observing how you and your spouse respond to each other. Don't feel that you have to "steal" a kiss when the kids aren't looking or save your caresses and romantic words for the bedroom. How long has it been since your teen has seen you get dressed up for a night out, complete with corsage and polished shoes? Is it out of character for you and your spouse to snuggle in front of the TV? It shouldn't be. Kids tend to mimic their parents. If you like romance with your spouse, your kids will try to find a marriage partner for similar enjoyment.

Second, talk candidly about homosexuality with your children *before* they are teens. Explain what it is and why it is wrong. Believe me, they hear about it at a very early age, but what they hear may not be what you want them to learn. They may think it is "weird," sort of like being lefthanded is unusual. Let them know it is more than weird—that it is *wrong*. On occasion, kids masturbate together. Some masturbate each other. These activities can open the door to gay fantasy and behavior. Yet only one in 1000 parents ever discusses masturbation with his children. What a mistake, because you can be sure that their friends talk about it with them.

Third, as old-fashioned as this sounds, a son needs time with his father and a daughter needs time with her mother. If you're a single mom with a son, please try to find a trustworthy male adult who can take the boy fishing or to a ball game. As boys learn about true manhood and girls learn about womanhood, they will develop a strong sense of identity, which in turn makes them less vulnerable to sex-role confusion.

Finally, know with whom your child spends the most time. Make sure that those persons are good influences. You are not being paranoid to question why a man would begin showing excessive interest in your son or why a woman invites your daughter over more than occasionally. To those in the gay community who insist that homosexuals aren't interested in recruiting juveniles, I say, Just read the newspaper. Hardly a month goes by without some tragic story of a trusted person's arraignment or conviction for molesting a younger person of the same sex.

Dad, I'm gay

Why is it that our kids don't come to us with questions about sex? Could it be that we've discouraged them by not listening when they have tough questions on other subjects? Would they really be able to come to you and say, "Mom, I think I might be a homosexual?" Have you dared think how you might handle such a question?

I am deeply concerned about the closeted homosexual activity on our Christian colleges and universities. In some cases it's not even closeted. This reveals that Christian families are not immune from having a member become a homosexual. I wish I were mistaken, but then again, why should we be surprised? Homosexual behavior is a sin, and the Bible shows us that sin visits the homes of the just as well as the unjust. It would be foolish to assume that you will never have to deal with homosexuality in your children.

Before we discuss ways to deal with homosexuality in your teen, let me briefly state my views on the subject. As a Christian I believe that homosexual behavior *is* a sin. In terms of homosexual orientation, I agree with those who say that it is a learned behavior, and I am highly skeptical of the research that suggests that in some cases there is a genetic predisposition to homosexuality. In either case we must treat the homosexual with love and understanding, always pointing toward celibacy and a rejection of the homosexual lifestyle. I also believe that through the power of the Holy Spirit and professional, biblically based counseling and therapy, a person with homosexual tendencies can be transformed. But such transformation is seldom "sudden." We do a disservice to glibly urge the homosexual to "pray for healing." He needs much more than that.

Now what about your son or daughter? What should you do if your teen has become involved in homosexual activity? By now, you know how much I believe in honest, loving communication. It is imperative in this situation that you be able to talk freely and lovingly with your child. Your teen may be acting out fantasies generated by the homoerotic media images that he or she has seen. That's certainly troublesome, but it may not mean that your teen is a homosexual. It may be more rebelliousness than sexual preference. It may also mean that your teen is curious. In either case it is important that you educate more than coerce. Try to talk about sexuality as a good gift from God that Satan will always attempt to destroy. You will, no doubt, be alarmed, but try not to show it. Help your teen see the big picture. Ask him to envision himself as a fifty-year-old. Tell her that curiosity about same-sex relationships is not that unusual and generally passes if we do not focus too much attention on it. Your goal is to diffuse the fascination with something that is currently in vogue within the alluring fields of music, movies, and fashion.

You may discern in talking together, however, that your teen has a more serious attraction to homosexuality. If that seems to be the case, please *listen* to your young person, who may really need to "pour it all out." *Listen*, no matter how difficult it is. And remember that healing from homosexuality is a long process that will require the best of your parenting skills. The following suggestions are not at all exhaustive but will help parents take the right first steps with their kids:

Tell them that you love them. Nearly all homosexual teens I've talked to say that they can't tell their parents because "they'd kill me." Imagine how startling it would be for you to greet their news with, "Tom, before I say anything else I want to tell you how much I love you." Say it and *mean* it. He is still your son—she is still your daughter. Hate the sin. Love the sinner.

Tell them why you believe that homosexuality is wrong. They need to see that your loving them does not mean that you approve of their behavior.

Tell them that God forgives them. Most homosexual teens I've talked with are lonely and guilt-ridden. They feel that they have committed an unpardonable sin, one reason why so many try suicide. One of the most important stages toward healing is to understand God's forgiveness.

Point out the risks. Explain to them that even so-called safe sex procedures can fail and that teenagers who are infected with AIDS in the '90s may not know or show evidence that they have the disease. Also, I highly recommend that you have them tested for HIV. Not only does this make good sense medically, but it makes a strong statement to them about the serious risks associated with their lifestyle.

Replace bad influences with good ones. It's very difficult getting a teen out of a destructive circle of peers, but one of the best replacements is a parent. Take a long weekend and go someplace special with your teen. Maybe he's always enjoyed spending time with a favorite grandparent or aunt—stop everything and visit them. A lot is at stake here, so the additional time and expense is worth it. Help your son or daughter to discard magazines and printed material that has encouraged them to explore homosexuality.

Seek professional help. Your pastor can help you locate counseling resources that combine the best of psychology and human development with biblical understanding. You and your spouse should also seek counsel and encouragement from your pastor and a close circle of Christian friends.

Try to get a commitment. If you have been able to apply the steps that I've outlined above, you are in a good position to ask your son or daughter to make a commitment to change. You have met your teen halfway. You have expressed your love and acceptance. You have laid a good foundation for being able to say, "Would you be willing at least to consider the possibility that your homosexuality will eventually make you very unhappy and could even kill you, but that it is possible to experience healing?"

Pray constantly. Make your son or daughter's sexual wholeness your number-one prayer. Spend time on your knees with your spouse. Ask your pastor to pray. Ask your close friends to pray. Unleash God's power in a way that you have never believed possible.

Let go. In spite of your efforts, your teen may still decide to adopt a homosexual lifestyle. Aside from the discipline you would impose on a heterosexual teen who is being promiscuous, it will not help to berate and harangue your teen. Express your disapproval. Uphold standards of behavior in your home. Continue to love. But be willing to turn your teen over completely to God's care and conviction. Albeit this is one of the hardest things for a parent to do, it may allow God to do what you are praying for him to do: heal your teen of homosexuality.

What do you know about AIDS?

How can I get AIDS?

The most common way HIV (the AIDS virus) is transmitted is through sexual activity in which the semen or blood of one infected person enters the bloodstream of another. This can happen through vaginal or anal sexual intercourse, in oral sex—with a man, or with a woman during her menses, or through sharing sex toys (such as a vibrator). It is not uncommon for there to be slight breaks in the lining of the mouth, vagina, or rectum that allow a passageway for the virus into the bloodstream.

HIV is also transmitted by drug users who share dirty needles and through blood transfusions with HIV positive blood (though this is now extremely rare since all blood donations are tested for HIV).

During pregnancy, females with AIDS may infect unborn children.

Do only homosexuals get AIDS?

No, although homosexuals form the highest percentage of AIDS victims at this time. However, AIDS can be contracted from heterosexual activity if one partner is infected.

Is there a cure for AIDS?

No.

Can you get AIDS by giving blood?

No. Clean needles are used whenever blood is donated.

Do condoms provide protection from AIDS?

Not entirely. Condoms occasionally break during sexual activity.

Can you visually detect if a person has AIDS?

No. A person may appear perfectly healthy and still be carrying the HIV virus.

Can you test negative and still have HIV? Yes. You may have been exposed recently enough that your body has not had time to produce antibodies.

5

ALCOHOL

"I want to stop drinking."

DEAR JERRY,

> I want to stop drinking but it seems impossible. Why is it so hard for me to stop? Am I an alcoholic? When I am not drinking I feel very lost and lonely and confused. This causes me to think about suicide. I've tried it five times.
>
> TRISTIN

▼▼▼▼▼▼▼▼▼▼▼▼▼▼

DEAR JERRY,

> I am 16 years old, and I have seen more and dealt with more than most people do in a lifetime. I'm an alcoholic, trying to battle my disease everyday. I was hospitalized twice in the same year for depression, suicide attempts, family problems, school problems,

and severe hostility. I began drinking when I was 11 years old.

ALICE

▼▼▼▼▼▼▼▼▼▼▼▼▼▼

DEAR JERRY,

I'm a 17 year old female who just graduated from high school. I prefer not to mention my name, but I'm commonly referred to as "speedy." (I'll let you use your imagination.) I'm not really into drugs unless you consider vodka a drug, which I'm sure you do. I'm not an alcoholic or anything like that, but if I'm going to a party, I'm gonna drink vodka. I used to think life was good, but as I get older I realize that everything I thought was good was really bad.

LORA

▼▼▼▼▼▼▼▼▼▼▼▼▼▼

DEAR JERRY JOHNSTON,

I feel like I'm the lowest person on earth. During my recent high school years I have gotten on drugs and quit that. Now I just drink. I'm really scared because lately I need a beer to have a good time. A good friend of mine says I'm on the verge of being an alcoholic. I can't talk to my parents because they are too busy. My dad's job has always been more important. Instead of love, to make up for his absence he bought me 2 cars, a boat, and anything else I say I want. Right now I am lonely and beer seems to be my best friend.

ROXANE

DEAR JERRY,

I am 14 and I think I'm an alcoholic. I don't drink a lot; just when I am around some friends of mine. I just started this summer. A friend of mine pressured me into it. My mother doesn't let me go out so I sneak out with my friend Missy. Missy ended up getting pregnant. But when she told her mom, she made her have an abortion. Missy has been real upset. And I am so sad.

JILL

▼▼▼▼▼▼▼▼▼▼▼▼▼

DEAR MR. JOHNSTON,

I am 14 years old. I am an alcoholic and I'm always depressed. I feel like no one really cares. It seems like no one knows how it feels to be empty, scared, and angry inside. I have had several sexual encounters with guys. I feel like a damn slut. I didn't intend to do it but I did it partly because I was drinking. My mom and dad think their little girl can do no wrong. Mom thinks I would never get drunk. What I am really asking is for someone to care enough to tell me they care. My parents never say "Dawnyel, I love you." I don't really like my parents.

DAWNYEL

▼▼▼▼▼▼▼▼▼▼▼▼▼

DEAR JERRY,

I am into alcohol and cigarettes and I can't stop. One of these days I'm going to come home drunk and my mom and I are going to get into a fight and I'm going to hit her. I don't want my mom to find out I drink.

GARTH

▼▼▼▼▼▼▼▼▼▼▼▼▼

One of the saddest by-products of our nation's thirst for alcohol is the sight of a teenager who is drunk. It isn't a pretty sight. Childlike eyes that ought to be opened to the joy of being young and innocent are glazed over from one-too-many beers sneaked out of a friend's refrigerator. Slurred speech that sounds incongruous comes from a voice that hasn't yet changed. Tender bodies still rounded with baby fat are retching next to a tree.

And perhaps the worst sight of all: lying on a covered gurney, a thirteen-year-old's lifeless form being carried away from a pile of metal and glass.

I have seen those sights and have talked with many more than Dawnyel and Roxanne. These are kids who might sit in your church's Sunday school class or baby-sit your children. They are frightened, lonely, and sad. They don't like what's happening to them but don't know what to do about it.

Alcohol is our nation's number one drug problem. To put that into perspective, let's take a look at the current scene.

The breweries want your kids

United States Surgeon General Antonia Novello is upset! She has targeted her anger at the alcoholic beverage industry, saying that it is time to stop using ads that feature sex, beauty, music, and fun, to "tantalize" America's youth into underage drinking. Surgeon General Novello's recent government survey reports that

- about 10,600,000 teens drink
- 8,000,000 drink weekly
- and almost a half-million indulge in weekly binge-drinking (five or more drinks in a row)

The report indicates that of those who drink, 25% drink to get high, 45% drink when they are upset, and 25% drink when they are bored.

Dr. Novello is correct in targeting the breweries and their advertising agencies. Your kids sit squarely in the sights of the makers of beverage alcohol. According to Jean Kilbourne of the National Council on Alcoholism, by age eighteen the average teen has seen 100,000 beer commercials on television. And the message those commercials send is always the same—that alcohol makes life better.

Stroh Brewery Company's "Old Milwaukee" beer is just one example. Its "Swedish Bikini Team," who also appeared in *Playboy* magazine, coyly tells the viewer, "It doesn't get any better than this." What teenage boy could ignore the implied connection between gorgeous women, good times, and beer? What girl wouldn't want to be in that scene with one of those tanned, muscular guys? Tom Pirko of Bevmark, a beverage-industry consulting firm notes, "You still basically have one ironclad attitude in the brewing industry, which is that you cannot sell beer effectively to young men unless you use sex."

That tactic seems to be working. In fact, the denotation of the verb "to drink" has become almost synonymous with the consuming of an alcoholic liquid. Almost every high school student in America has tried alcohol. The National Institute of Drug Abuse makes it clear that the number of teens who use drugs has always been much lower than the number of those who drink. Nine out of ten high school seniors have tried alcohol, and 60% of those seniors are current users (compared with 14% who use marijuana).

I have spoken in almost 4,000 high schools, and in every one of them I have listened to tragic stories caused by alcohol abuse. The kids all know friends who are either already dead because of an alcohol-related traffic accident or who are hopelessly hooked on alcohol. When I spoke at Omaha's Ralston High School, a special bell tolled periodically over the school's intercom system, representing another death brought on by alcohol. Some of the students dressed in black, their faces painted a ghastly white. These grim reapers stalked the school throughout the day seeking new prey that symbolically mirrored the loss of young life from the most lethal liquid in America. As part of an alcohol awareness program, these students wanted to rescue their classmates from the bondage of their drinking.

The statistics beyond fatalities are staggering—18% of all people grow up with an alcoholic or a problem drinker; of separated and divorced people under forty-five, two-thirds of the women and one-half of the men had alcoholism in their families. Children of alcoholics are at greater risk of having psychological problems and difficulty with intimacy in relationships when they become adults.

I wish that this forty-four billion dollar industry would read some of the letters I receive from fourteen-year-old alcoholics—that they would listen to the sobbing of a youngster who can't enjoy anything without first having a few beers. The production and distribution of alcohol is big business, and to keep the stream of customers flowing, the breweries are "talking" to your kids. But *who's listening?*

What about your *kids?*

If you have a child who is more than twelve years old, I can promise you one thing: He or she has already been in a situation where alcohol was available and the temptation to drink was pronounced, because by the time kids reach high school they face almost irresistible pressure to drink. Most kids, in fact, start drinking not because they want to but because they are pressured into it.

Consider this scenario: Your thirteen-year-old daughter has been invited to a sleep-over at a friend's house. You know the family and consent to let her go.

When your daughter arrives at her friend's house, she runs upstairs and notices that her friend is giggling a little more than usual. Soon your daughter finds out why. Her friend pulls open a dresser drawer to reveal a bottle of vodka that she swiped from her dad's bar in the rec room. "You mix it with orange juice, and no one knows— you can't smell it on your breath. Here have some." Your daughter has been taught to stay away from alcohol and drugs, but somehow this seems so harmless. Besides, she doesn't want to seem like a prude, so she accepts the glass and promises herself never to drink again.

For guys, accepting a drink is something of a rite of passage. Somebody gets an older brother to buy a six-pack. You all meet at a vacant lot next to the park. The bottles get passed around and you *know* that you will not be able to say no. The guy that turns down a beer is a wimp. Who wants to be a wimp?

This is the world your teenagers live in. This is what they face practically every day. When they leave the house for school each day, you ought to say a prayer for them. But you can do more.

Know the terrain. The best way to keep your teens sober is to help them stay away from alcohol. It sounds simple, but it's true. Know who their friends are. Keep your "ear to the ground" regarding the big parties. Don't let your teens work in businesses that sell or serve alcohol. If you are a social drinker, ask yourself this question: How would I feel if my son or daughter got drunk on my beer and drove into another car? Your occasional beer or cocktail may not be worth the risk of the damage it could do to your kids.

Give them excuses to stay sober. If your teen begins hanging out with known drinkers, or pressures you to let him go to a party where you know that alcohol will be served, don't just give a lecture about abstinence. Give something better: "Hey Tim, I love you too much to let you ride in a car with a guy who will probably be drunk by the end of the night. Why don't you tell him you can't go because you're going fishing with me?" Then *take him* fishing.

Get involved in your teen's world. I'm in total agreement with high school principals who tell parents to call hosts of teen parties to ask if alcohol will be served. Join with other parents and pledge to keep all socials alcohol-free. And volunteer to chaperone school social events and trips. Too often, Christian parents are quick to criticize high school socials when we should be present as positive influences.

Keep them busy. Remember: One of the reasons that kids drink is that they're bored. Promote and encourage participation in extra-curricular activities. Show interest in the things that your teen is interested in. Plan outings around your teen's interests. Let her bring her friends over and don't be too strict about the loudness of their music or the rowdiness of their behavior (better in your house than someone else's).

Take the glamour out of drinking. Whenever you read an account of an alcohol-related fatality in your local newspaper, share it with your teen. Help your teen to see that alcohol is almost always related to tragedy. If you live near a rescue mission, plan a visit. The sight of men and women who've lost it all to alcohol can be a powerful object lesson.

Don't ignore the hints. The very first time you suspect that your son or daughter has been drinking, don't ignore it. But don't panic, either. This is *not* the time to start an argument. In all likelihood your teen has been pressured for a long time and has finally given in. Let mercy temper your disappointment. Build him up: "*You* know you made a mistake and so do we, but we still love you. Encourage her: "You'll be stronger next time." Guide him: "What can we do to help you stay away from drinking?" Discipline her: "To help you understand how serious this is, you will not be allowed to go out with your friends for two weeks."

Show that you care. Many kids drink because they think that their parents don't care. *Show* that *you* do. Talk to them specifically about drinking. Without being threatening, ask them to tell you about the drinking scene at their school. Let them know that they can talk to you about it without getting a lecture. Communication (see Chapter 12) will go a long way toward keeping your teen sober.

Your reaction to your teen's *experimenting* with alcohol will help determine his future choices, but if your child continues beyond a first or second occasion of drinking, take it seriously. Don't wish it away. I've talked with many parents who wish that they had intervened earlier. And I've talked with teens who say that they wouldn't be in such bad shape if their parents had done something— besides get mad—to keep them sober. I know that it's not easy. Because we have invested so greatly in our children, it sometimes makes us angry to see them take steps down a destructive pathway. But if we keep a lid on our anger and focus solely on the task of helping our child stay away from alcohol, we will see rewarding results.

One of the first things you should do if you suspect that your child has a drinking problem is to have a heart-to-heart conversation in which you tell him that you are going to make his sobriety your priority. He might deny that he has a problem or may ask you to stay out of his life, but deep down inside will be glad to see that you care enough to try.

I also recommend getting help. Call or visit your teen's school counselor and explain your concern. Ask about resources to help you work with your teen. Many schools have excellent peer counseling programs that match up positive teen role models with younger kids just starting to develop a drinking problem. Alcohol counseling units at community hospitals have become a growth industry, and that's because they achieve results. It may be what your son or daughter needs to turn the corner. You might also consider finding an ally in another adult whom your teen respects—a youth pastor, a coach, or a favorite aunt or uncle. The point is, don't try to go it alone. It seldom works.

As you work with your teen to help him conquer his drinking problem, reward sobriety. Every time that your teen goes out socially you can bet that he has been offered a chance to drink. Acknowledge that and give verbal pats on the back for standing up to the temptation. Make a big deal about such success because it *is* a big deal.

Do as you say

Above all, don't be a hypocrite. Kids hate that. If you are a social drinker, maybe you should stop. Your child's sobriety is important enough for you to give up your nightcap, isn't it? This will make a dramatic statement to your teen.

I'm not hesitant at all to say that I am an abstainer. I watched alcohol almost destroy my own mom. Before God delivered her, she was averaging a quart of vodka a day. Through the power of prayer she was delivered and can say today, "God took the desire for alcohol away."

I don't ever want my kids to see their dad drunk. Not only will they lose respect for me—they themselves will be more likely to drink, because kids will mimic their parents. If you drink, chances are that they will too—that's been proven. *Model* for them. *Inform* them. *Lead* them. Most of all, create in your home an atmosphere in which no teen will be motivated to drink. The environment in your home can be the greatest determinant for your teen in discovering how empty drinking really is.

Remember how the evil King Nebuchadnezzar tried to change Daniel: One of his attempts was to get Daniel drunk. My favorite verse in the Old Testament, Daniel 1:8, states: "But Daniel made up his mind that he would not defile himself with the king's choice food or with the wine which he drank" (NASB).

Daniel made up his mind. Help your teen make that same commitment.

6

ABORTION

"I decided to get an abortion."

DEAR JERRY,

I wish I was dead. One night this summer I snuck out of the house and went to a party with a friend. I got drunk and ended up getting pregnant and then got an abortion. I never thought I'd do anything like that. My mom doesn't know about it and I don't want her to 'cuz all she'd do is put me down more. I want someone to love me, care about me. I want someone to talk to about different fun stuff. I want to be happy. I don't want to hurt anymore!

KATIE

▼▼▼▼▼▼▼▼▼▼▼▼▼

JERRY,

I'm 17 years old and a senior in high school. I was pregnant a month or so ago. I had nowhere to turn. My parents knew and the father knew. I felt like dropping all the pressure that was bringing me down. I felt it was my duty to control myself but couldn't, so I attempted suicide. Everyone suddenly payed more attention to me except my boyfriend. He deceived me in so many ways so I broke up with him. Now was the time for decision making. I decided to get an abortion. My doctor sent me to a fine clinic near Dallas. It was a Monday when we went. The doctor examined me and told my father I may be too far along. So we went for a second opinion.

GINGER

DEAR JERRY,

I'm 15 years old and I've made two suicide attempts. To other people I guess my life looked pretty good. Good grades, friends, serious boyfriend. But Richard and I started having problems. The drugs and alcohol I used to have a good time started to become something I used to "get away." Then I got pregnant. Perfect timing, huh? I knew I couldn't take care of a child, but how could I kill my baby? I cried for so long. Richard convinced me to get an abortion. He came from a broken home and told me it wouldn't be right to bring an unwanted baby into the world. And I just couldn't carry a baby nine months and then just give it away. Richard and I fell apart two weeks later. One night I came home stoned and drunk, sliced my wrists, and lay down on my bed. My parents found me and I spent two weeks in a psychiatric ward. My psychiatrist is helping me deal with the guilt from my baby. I just wanted to tell you.

JULIA

▼▼▼▼▼▼▼▼▼▼▼▼▼▼

DEAR JERRY JOHNSTON,

Last June I got pregnant. I was afraid when I discovered my pregnancy that it would disappoint my Christian parents. So I talked to my boyfriend and opted for an abortion. All my life I had said I would stay a virgin until marriage and that I would never have an abortion. How things change. But after reading your book and doing some soul searching I decided to cancel my appointment for an abortion and go through with having my baby. As I look upon my beautiful three-month-old daughter I can't believe that almost a year ago her life could have been terminated just like that. Thank you for writing *Going All the Way.*

HEIDI

▼▼▼▼▼▼▼▼▼▼▼▼▼▼

Every twenty-one seconds a baby is aborted. One hundred and seventy abortions are performed every hour; 4,100 every day; 29,000 every week; 125,000 a month.

The most recent year for statistics available in the United States revealed that 1.4 million abortions were performed in twelve months. Since *Roe v. Wade*, the landmark Supreme Court decision legalizing abortion in 1973, more than 26,000,000 abortions have been performed in the United States—the equivalent of Canada's entire population!

Many of those abortions were performed on teenage girls. *One* of those abortions could have been performed

81

on your daughter without your ever knowing it. That's entirely possible, for in some states parents do not have to give consent for their daughters to obtain abortions. Think of it: Your daughter needs your permission to have her ears pierced but can go to the local abortion clinic and have a fetus removed from her womb and killed! Before you are too quick to blame the legislatures for passing such insane laws, consider that many parents are so distant from their teens that a girl could become pregnant and have an abortion without their knowing it.

Talk about a lack of communication: I know of a girl who had an abortion, showed up for dinner looking pale and without an appetite, and her folks never noticed!

Have you noticed a pattern in the letters I shared at the beginning of this chapter? Most of them mentioned suicide. Every young girl I've talked to who's had an abortion has considered suicide. Her guilt is so strong that she wants out. This and a dead baby are the legacy of the so-called "pro-choice movement." I find it ironic that our society emphasizes choice and rights so strongly without informing people of the emotional baggage that comes from choosing an abortion.

In the case of many young girls who find themselves pregnant, however, "choice" is hardly the right word to apply to their decisions to terminate their pregnancies. Usually the first bit of loving guidance from the young man who got them pregnant is "Hey, we're not ready to be parents. Why don't you just get an abortion?" Then he leaves her. Now put yourself in her shoes. What would you do?

Are you encouraging abortion?

Frequently I talk with young girls from strict, religious homes whose parents let them know by word and action that an out-of-wedlock pregnancy is an unpardonable sin. When a girl in this situation gets pregnant, her first thought is to make sure that no one finds out. And we all know that there's only one way to do that. Inwardly, she would like to give birth to the baby and is often idealistic enough to imagine keeping it, but her fear of disappointing Mom and Dad is so great that she opts for an abortion. She goes to Planned Parenthood, makes an appointment with a clinic they recommend, shows up in the morning, and goes home at night no longer pregnant but burdened with almost unbearable sadness and guilt.

How sad. But it happens. We can let our distaste for sin become so pronounced that the sinner feels hated. In this case, the "sinner" is a young daughter who feels that she's at the end of her rope. Her boyfriend may have left her after finding out about the pregnancy. Life as a young mother scares her. She feels as if all her plans will be derailed by her pregnancy. And she is scared to death of what her parents will say if they find out. Is this teenager capable of making a wise choice? Does she even *have* a choice?

I hope that you have talked lovingly with your daughter about sexuality. I hope that you have encouraged her to remain a virgin until she marries, and I hope that your daughter has made that wonderful commitment. But I think it would also be wise for you to talk with your daughter about "what if?" I hope that she knows that if she were to become pregnant that you would want to be the first to know and that you would support her carrying the baby to full term. I am convinced that fewer teens would seek abortions if they had had these kinds of conversations with their parents.

If your daughter becomes pregnant, you can help her see that abortion will not help but will actually make things worse. Here's what I recommend:

Be quick to forgive. Believe me, she already feels terrible, so spare her the sermon. In fact, her guilt could be so strong that without your knowing it she may be planning an abortion. How you respond may convince her that the best thing to do is to get rid of the baby as quickly as possible. Smother her with love and forgiveness.

Discourage her from a premature marriage. The old "shotgun wedding" almost always ends in divorce. Unless you discern a mature love between your daughter and the baby's father, dissuade her from a marriage of convenience. The younger she (and he) is, the more important it is that you help her avoid marriage.

Encourage her to have the baby. This should be a given, right from the beginning. Don't be afraid to use the word "baby." That's what it is. If your daughter mentions the possibility of an abortion, don't throw a fit. Remind her that abortion will end the life of the baby inside her. Show her pictures of a fetus, letting her see that the "lump" inside of her has already begun to form. Promise her that you will stand beside her emotionally and financially if she decides to keep the baby. Keep in mind that others may be counseling her to have an abortion. Anger will only drive her closer to these counselors, whereas love, acceptance, and forgiveness will make your position more compelling.

Get help from allies. Contact your local chapter of the National Right to Life Committee or other pro-life agencies and explain your situation to them. They can be extremely helpful in providing counseling for your daughter. One of the best deterrents to abortion is to have your daughter talk to another girl who has had an abortion and believes that she made a serious mistake. Such a girl is not hard to find.

Help her obtain prenatal care. Because of the parents' embarrassment and the daughter's ignorance, proper health care is often neglected with the pregnant teenager. Your family physician can recommend a qualified gynecologist.

Help her move from despair to hope. A child will soon be born. In the right environment it will grow up healthy and strong and will bring joy to many people. Help your daughter see that God is in the business of redeeming our mistakes.

In my opinion, the absolute best decision your daughter can make is to give birth to the baby and then offer it for adoption. Consult your pastor or family physician to learn more about agencies that help place infants in loving adoptive homes, or call 1-800-BETHANY, a Christian agency that can recommend other avenues for adoption.

I hope that your daughter will agree that adoption is the best choice. She may, however, decide that she wants to keep the baby and marry the father, or keep the baby and raise it as a single mom. As unwise and unrealistic as this might be, take comfort in the fact that your daughter has chosen life! Then explore ways you can help her make the very best of her decision. Teen marriages from unexpected pregnancies have one of the highest rates of divorce in the nation, but they *can* survive if they receive support from family and church. And although a child raised by a single mom faces serious challenges, loving grandparents can help fill the void of not having a father.

My point is this: The church has been very vocal in its opposition to abortion, without providing alternatives to young women in trouble. If the only option that we "sanction" is adoption, we had better face the reality that some girls would rather abort their child than give it up. If we are truly pro-life, we will support any decision that results in the baby's being allowed to live.

A special word to sons

As you may have noticed, everything I've written so far has been aimed at daughters. Unfortunately, that's the way society—especially the church—treats teen pregnancy—as the girl's problem. The guy who *got* her pregnant moves on with his life intact while the girl struggles alone with some pretty heavy decisions. That's not fair, nor is it right. I believe that there would be far fewer abortions if men faced up to their responsibilities as the biological father of a child.

If your son is responsible for getting a girl pregnant, help him face up to his actions. But handle this in the same manner I've recommended that you treat your daughter should she become pregnant. Make sure that he knows that he is loved and forgiven. So many times we let our disappointment drive a wedge between us and our children. Your son will already know that he has made a serious mistake. Show him that he is forgiven, that there is a right way to proceed, and that you will walk that path with him.

This would be an excellent time to ask your son what he plans to do about the baby. Again, use the word *baby*. He needs to think in terms of a living, breathing child, not just an inanimate result of his mistake. He may need to be introduced to some options (you would be surprised how little a young man thinks about the results of sexual experimentation). He may genuinely believe that he and his girlfriend are in love and ready for marriage. If that's the case, talk with him about the challenges of marriage and family at such a young age. More likely, your son will want to find the easiest and quickest way out of his dilemma. Point out that he already has done something that was "easy" when he gave in to sexual temptation. The easy way didn't help him then and won't help him now. Far better to do the *right* thing, which is to make sure the baby is given the best possible start in life.

Encourage your son to share in any medical expense that comes with a woman's carrying a baby to full term. That includes prenatal care, something that is usually avoided in teen pregnancies. Explain to your son that if his girlfriend begins seeing a physician right away, she will have a much easier delivery and the baby will have a better chance of entering the world in good health. Your goal is to make sure that your son is convinced that the baby must be born—that he will not pressure his girlfriend to seek an abortion.

After you have discussed the issues with your son, the very next thing he should do, in my opinion, is to make sure that the girl's parents know that he will take responsibility for his actions. Ideally, he should make an effort to apologize to the girl's parents and let them know that he will share the responsibility of making the right decisions regarding the child he has fathered. Now that's a very tough assignment, and in some cases it might not be possible. For example, the girl's parents might be so angry that they do not want to even *see* your son again. If that's the case, encourage your son to at least send a letter. By acknowledging his actions and facing up to his responsibility, he will be paving the way for real healing to take place. It also helps make abortion seem like an unnecessary action, keeping in mind that many teen abortions come from attempts to keep the pregnancy a secret.

What if?

Suppose that you've tried everything I've suggested and your daughter ultimately decides to have an abortion. Depending on her age, she may legally have that right. What do you do as a parent?

Believe me, I hope that you never have to face such a possibility, because it will place you in between your love for your daughter and your heartfelt convictions. Do you assist your daughter in finding a clinic that will perform the abortion? Or do you leave her on her own to be counseled and assisted by people whose beliefs and values are directly opposed to your own? Do you walk through the "valley of the shadow of death" with your daughter or do you send her packing?

These are some of the most difficult questions a parent can face, and I cannot answer them for you. I raise them because any of us with daughters could have them looming over our heads. Perhaps just thinking about them now will convince you of the urgency in making sure that your daughter understands the value of human life. Perhaps imagining such a dilemma will lead you to spend more time listening to your daughter *before* it's too late.

Moms and Dads, stay close to your daughters once they begin dating. Talk openly about love, sex, and abortion with your children and their boyfriends and girlfriends. Give them opportunities to ask questions and share their feelings. Utilize one of the many videos available on the consequences of abortion and watch it together. Follow it up with a very frank discussion.

I don't believe that abortion has to happen. Our kids are smarter and more logical than we give them credit for being—but only when they are given the facts about abortion. If we don't educate them properly, they will most likely do what the many gifted counselors in the pro-choice movement tell them to do. Can you blame them?

Make sure that your teenager knows that abortion is such a lousy option that it's not an option at all.

7

DRUG ABUSE

"The drugs just took over."

DEAR JERRY,

I was 15 when I got started on cocaine. It was the first drug I ever used. I quickly went on to a synthetic drug: crystal. Not that many months later I overdosed, almost losing my life. After the rehabilitation center where I stayed until I was kicked out early, I went back home feeling so hopeless I had no desire to live. From using drugs my health had gotten really bad. I had to go to the hospital with a throat condition and it was to the point where I could hardly breath. I went back to my old school and did good for a while but I got back into drugs by a girl who was taking me to group therapy and Narcotics Anonymous. This time it was much worse. I got directly involved with drug dealers and since I wasn't spending my own money and could have all I wanted, the drugs just took over. I started freebasing, I weighed 100 pounds. I started running away and staying in drug houses, motels, and the streets. Then I went to a shelter and accepted Jesus and I meant it in my heart. My old desires went away.

GAIL

▼▼▼▼▼▼▼▼▼▼▼▼▼▼

DEAR JERRY,

I'm sixteen years old. I have been a brilliant student all my life. I'm what you call a nerd who knows everything from A to Z. I started to feel lonely and helpless because I didn't know anyone in school and also the nerds wouldn't talk to me. So I did cocaine and all my problems went away so fast and I felt so good I felt like having more and after a few months passed I realized that my attendance and grades were so bad I felt even more helpless. All of my dreams were gone. I wanted to go to the university but now I can't. I feel no good. I'm nothing anymore. I'm just a stupid junkie.

ADRIAN

▼▼▼▼▼▼▼▼▼▼▼▼▼▼

DEAR MR. JOHNSTON,

I have done everything from smoking pot to shooting heroin. Since the age of 13 it's been hell on earth. I was raped at 12 years of age. Did so badly in school I barely passed that year. I've been a prostitute. I've taken speed and snorted crystal and shot up until January this year. I've gone cold turkey until I can't stand it anymore then I start all over again. I get so

sick and hallusinate so I give up. Somehow I feel you
will read this and have some answers.

PORTIA

DEAR JERRY,

See when I was 7 years old I found out that the man
I thought was my father wasn't. He thought I was
his kid also. Anyways my stepfather was beating me
up all the time so I turned to drugs to make the pain
go away. I got real serious with a guy. I was fixin' to
get married but he died in a four-car collision. You
made me realize that I don't need drugs to make the
pain stop. All I have to do is ask the Lord for help and
he'll do his best.

DAPHNE

DEAR JERRY,

I'm 18 years old, and I've been into just about every
drug and crime you can think of. The last 5 years of
my life have been a tormented hell for myself and everyone around me. Right now I'm in jail. I've just finished reading your book. Please help me.

LANCE

DEAR JERRY,

I left home at 15. Ran away from some heavy abuse
in an alcoholic and highly dysfunctional family. I
went to Las Vegas, Denver, Albuquerque, and finally

came back to the streets. I have been addicted to cocaine and heroin since before I left home.

CORA

▼▼▼▼▼▼▼▼▼▼▼▼▼

DEAR JERRY,

I was the kid who always got beat up in school. It got
so bad I would act sick so I wouldn't have to go to
school. I got a job working in a soft drink place so
with money came drugs and with drugs came power,
girl friends, and more money. It was so easy to skip
school. The teachers didn't care. They were just glad
I wasn't there. By the time I was 16 I began to do
coke. I went through 3 grams of coke, 100 hits of
LSD, and 12 grams of hash. I have seen a couple of
good friends die. Pray for me. I don't think I can hang
on much longer. Help me find peace.

MARTY

▼▼▼▼▼▼▼▼▼▼▼▼▼

Remember when you were in high school and some of
the braver guys, if they were lucky, got their hands on a
six-pack of beer and got drunk after the homecoming
game? Maybe one of the really bad kids had tried marijuana?

Welcome to the nineties, where at every high school
you can find any illegal drug you want. Middle schools,
too, are becoming hot markets for the drug trade, and it
is not unusual for drugs to be present in elementary
schools as well. According to a survey conducted by the
U.S. Department of Health and Human Services, the
most readily available drug on high school campuses is
marijuana, followed by amphetamines, cocaine, crack,
tranquilizers, and LSD.

If you think that drugs are only an inner-city problem, forget it. Principals in suburban and rural schools
tell me horror stories of the high incidence of drug usage
in their schools. A detective in a comfortable Chicago sub-
urb recounted how he believes that drugs may be *more* of
a problem in the suburbs than downtown because "these
suburban kids have the money." My own experience as a
visitor to more than 3000 schools in America has convinced me that the drug problem cuts across all socio-
economic and geographical boundaries. If you have a son
or daughter in middle school or high school, you can be
reasonably certain that your child has been confronted
with drugs.

Why your child might try drugs

You would think all the excellent anti-drug efforts
would convince your teen that drugs are a dead-end
street. Yet new clients are being recruited every day for
the drug trade. Why would a clean-cut kid who plays varsity football and gets decent grades—a young woman
with a bright future ahead of her—why would your son or
daughter get sucked into the hellish prison of drug
abuse?

Three factors stand out in my mind as I talk with
kids who are either current drug users or who have successfully kicked the drug habit: peer pressure, poor self-
esteem, and boredom. Any one of these factors is signifi-
cant enough to lead a teen into drug usage, but in many
cases kids deal with all three—a dangerous combination.

Just say no . . . and be a real nerd

What too many of us forget is that one of the worst
things for a teenager is to be different. To stand out from
the crowd. If his peers like the heavy-metal group, Metallica, *he* likes Metallica. If your daughter's friends all wear
L.A. Gear running shoes, *she* wouldn't be caught dead in

Nikes. While this has always been true for teenagers, the pressure to conform to the group now seems stronger than ever before. As a parent you must understand this tremendous power because it is working overtime on your kids. It regularly makes your sons or daughters do things they really don't want to do, and this is especially true for kids who have a low self-esteem.

Just imagine what's running through your child's mind when he gets in his buddy's car after football practice and all his teammates in the car are passing around a joint. He knows that using drugs is wrong. He may have taken a pledge to remain drug-free. He would love to be strong enough to "just say no."

But he can't. In that awful moment he will most likely do something that violates his own values—all because of the power of peer pressure.

That's why it is so important for you as a parent to know who your teen's friends are. Nurture relationships with kids who don't use drugs. Talk with your child about peer pressure and of the importance of having *real* friends—kids who would never ask others to do something that's harmful or illegal. Peer pressure can work in their favor if they surround themselves with friends who are determined to stay drug-free. Help your children come up with "face-saving" lines that they can use when confronted by peers who offer them drugs:

"I would, but it might ruin my chances to become president some day."

"I better not. That stuff makes me puke."

"Call me stupid, but I really believe that stuff about fried brains."

Just trying to be somebody

Peer pressure is much less powerful with kids who have a clear sense of who they are. The teen with good self-esteem is the teen who has no problem saying *no* to anyone who offers her drugs, but for the teen who feels inferior, the invitation to join the group and take drugs is almost irresistible. Easy prey for a high school drug dealer is a new kid who is neither handsome, pretty, or especially gifted in sports or other popular activities. Any child who is uncomfortable with his appearance or who does not see himself as popular will be likely to try drugs if approached. In the youth subculture, drug usage is associated with popularity, with "coolness." The message from dealers is clear and appealing: "Try some of this and you'll be one of us. Part of the right group." That's music to the ears of those with poor self-esteem.

Too much time and money

Boredom, too, is a major factor in drug use among teens. This is especially true in upper middle-class suburban environments. Kids there have it fairly easy. They don't work. School doesn't challenge them. Passive interests such as television, music, and video games wear thin after a while. No one is home, but even when everyone *is* home, not much happens between parent and child except an argument. How many times do we hear kids say, "There's nothin' to do"?

When teens are bored, it's natural for them to try to fill that emptiness, and the easy availability of drugs becomes awfully tempting. Remember, these are kids who have seen through the hypocrisy of their parents' social drinking. If a cocktail before dinner is okay for Mom and Dad, then snorting a line of cocaine during lunch hour is fine for me. It's what I need to get through this boring day.

Peer pressure. Poor self-esteem. Boredom. No doubt that one of those factors touches your child every day. Try this activity. Mentally walk alongside your teenager from the time he leaves the house in the morning until he bolts through the door after school. If one of his friends offers him a pill "that will keep you sharp," will he accept it?

Will he cave in to the pressure of his friends who have been after him for months to try drugs? Does she have a strong enough sense of who she is to be able to say no? Is his life filled with wholesome activities and interests that make drugs seem terribly unattractive? If not, you need to consider your role in helping your teen deal with these factors that lead to drug use.

Be your teen's ally against drugs

Maybe you've seen this commercial on television: A father is having what seems to be an intimate conversation with his son and everything seems to be okay until the camera backs away to offer a wider angle. Dad's in a cemetery. As the narrator tells parents to talk to their kids about drugs, we realize that the cemetery holds the treasured son.

For *that* dad, it was too late. But it's not for *you*. One of the best ways to counter the effects of peer pressure, poor self-esteem, and boredom is to be a true *friend* to your teen. Keep communication lines open (see chapter 12). Spend time with your son or daughter. And *listen*. I don't know how many times I hear kids tell me that their parents never listen. If you haven't been a good listener, start now. It's a great hedge against poor self-esteem. By listening, you show that you care. You are really saying, "You're somebody special." When that message is consistent and continual, kids don't need to accept drugs to be accepted. Their parents have boosted their self-esteem simply by listening.

One of the toughest things for a parent to do is try to influence a son's or daughter's choice of friends. Often, we are wise to notice some friendships that develop with the wrong kind of people, but we don't quite know how to intervene. We either ignore the problem and hope that it will work itself out, or we create barriers by nagging our kids to drop a friendship. Neither option is helpful.

As far as I'm concerned, the best thing that you can do to help your child avoid the pressure (by "friends") to try drugs is to keep talking and listening. Take an interest in *all* their friends. Encourage your teens to bring their friends over after school. If you sense that one of their friends is up to no good, talk to your teen as if he is your best friend ("I've heard that Tim has a drug problem. Would he let you take the rap if you got pulled over and the officer found drugs in the car?"). Lots of decent kids have an altruistic motive in befriending someone with problems. They think that they can be a positive influence on them, and maybe they can. Don't discourage this sincere desire to help, but remind them that they will only be able to help as long as they themselves stay clean.

Perhaps the best defense against these three factors that lead to drug use is a tight-knit family. Surveys show that a strong, loving bond between children and their parents helps to prevent kids from bonding with their peers and succumbing to peer pressure. Strong families enhance self-esteem—if your child is secure with his place in your heart, he will not be as apt to desire the "popularity" promised by the drug crowd. I've also found that kids from strong families have fewer problems with boredom. When I look into the vacant eyes of a teenage drug abuser, I often wonder what might have happened if his father had taken him fishing occasionally; if her mother had played tennis with her regularly.

The teen years go by so quickly. Don't be like the father who started talking to his son after it was too late. *Start today to become your child's true friend.*

Is your teen using drugs?

Some of you reading this book may have already discovered that your son or daughter is using drugs. Everything I've written in this chapter still holds true for you. That is, perhaps more than ever before, your teen needs you to be a friend. Your child needs to see that you disapprove of the drug use, but that you do not disapprove of him or her. Smother your child in love—tough love when necessary—but always love. Listen more than talk. Hand out hugs with abandon. Walk with your teen along the difficult road to recovery.

The usual reaction from parents, I have observed, is embarrassment. Mom and Dad at first don't want to admit their son or daughter has a drug problem. Once they face that fact, they tend to withdraw from their familiar circles of friends and almost hide their wayward child. Nothing could be worse. By your own example, show your teen that facing a problem is better than running from it. Get help! Don't be ashamed to call the local mental health center in your city and schedule an appointment with their drug abuse counselors. And please, be willing to go with your teen to such helpful resources available in your community. The more upbeat and positive you are, the more that your child will begin to see that there is hope. That your love is *unconditional*.

Avoid the tendency to blame yourself—or your teen. Certainly you may have contributed to your teen's drug problem by being too busy or not sensitive enough or whatever. But it does little good to dwell on the past. The more you focus on the negatives, the wider the gap between you and your child will be. Before true healing can begin, you may, in fact, need to go up to your teen and acknowledge your shortcomings. Kids yearn for transparency in their role models. They will be more forgiving than you expect, opening up lines of communication that may not have existed for years.

Finally, don't neglect the spiritual dimensions of a drug problem. Is your own walk with God intact? Are you able to talk about your faith with your teen? Do you pray regularly for your teen to be victorious over drugs? Have you ever prayed with your son or daughter about this problem? It has been said that when the praying starts, the shouting stops. Faith in God is no guarantee that you and your family will not experience the tragedy of a drug problem, but faith gives a powerful resource to bring about recovery and wholeness. Lean heavily on your faith.

Christian parents have a tendency to think that their children are immune to the appeal of drugs. We act as if our faith has given us automatic protection from this serious national tragedy. That just isn't true. Many of the kids I talk to who are addicted to drugs come from Christian homes. It is not unusual to have pastors approach me in the cities where I'm speaking and confide to me that their son or daughter is heavily involved with drugs.

Don't make the mistake of thinking that it could never happen in your family. Face the reality: Your child will have access to drugs. Then face up to your responsibility as a parent. Be a true friend. Make time for companionship. And even when you're too tired or angry or at the end of your patience, *listen*. Always listen.

8

SATANISM

"I pray to Satan."

DEAR JERRY,

I was born into satanism by my parents. My father was a pedophile and a satanist. My mother was and may still be a satanist. I have witnessed children die by stabbings and gunfire. If you have a gun put to your head and refuse to have sex . . . well, it's curtains for that kid. I have also endured child pornography, incest, and child prostitution.

ANDY

DEAR JERRY,

I have been wondering if someone can get into satanism without really realizing they are. A friend of mine is very obsessed with black clothing. The state-

ment she uses most of the time is "sex is power."
Should I be worried about her or not?

SONYA

▼ ▾ ▼ ▾ ▼ ▾ ▼ ▾ ▼ ▾ ▼ ▾ ▼

DEAR MR. JOHNSTON,

I am seventeen and for the last year and a half I've
been in the occult. I am now attempting to escape.
It's so hard. For a little over a month I've been followed, threatened, beaten up, and tormented. Is that
how God works? I still see the demons in my house,
in my car. At first I loved the power, the drugs, the
money, the sex, but now it's miserable. When we sac-
rificed something everyone drank the blood and
sometimes I'll taste it again. How do I escape?

BILL

▼ ▾ ▼ ▾ ▼ ▾ ▼ ▾ ▼ ▾ ▼ ▾ ▼

DEAR MR. JOHNSTON,

Since I was a little girl I've always wanted to be a
witch, and I would read anything I could get my
hands on that dealt with satanism and witchcraft. I
believe in God and I believe he is the ruler of the
earth, not Satan. I am just so fascinated by all this.
I also like cemeteries. I was born on Halloween at 15
minutes before midnight.

ASHLEY

▼ ▾ ▼ ▾ ▼ ▾ ▼ ▾ ▼ ▾ ▼ ▾ ▼

DEAR JERRY,

I've really gotten into the occult and I don't want to
get in further, but I keep feeling pulled in like magic.
My room used to be a shrine of heavy-metal thunder

gods, but my mom trashed it. When I play music by Wasp, Mettalica, Megadeath, and Ozzy Osborn I feel like I'm being talked to and I feel like I should follow their directions. I'm scared.

HEIDI

▼▼▼▼▼▼▼▼▼▼▼▼▼

DEAR MR. JOHNSTON,

I haven't killed anyone yet, but I pray to Satan. People at school call me a witch. In some ways I am. I first discovered Satan a few years ago. Praying to him seems easier than praying to God. The other night I was drunk and I decided to talk to Satan, and he listened to me. He loves me. Please help me.

BRENDA

▼▼▼▼▼▼▼▼▼▼▼▼▼

DEAR JERRY,

I am 16 and my boyfriend is 21. He used to be into all those games like Dungeons and Dragons and black magic and now he has led me to believe there is no heaven or hell. I have tried to talk with him about God but he just says all humans are stupid, especially about religion. Please help me.

SUMMER

▼▼▼▼▼▼▼▼▼▼▼▼▼

DEAR JERRY,

When I was 13 I decided to worship Satan to make God mad at me or pay him back. Soon after I became highly aggressive. I am fighting suicidal urges after being raped recently by my ex-boyfriend.

BRIDGET

▼▼▼▼▼▼▼▼▼▼▼▼▼

103

From Los Angeles, California, to Frankfurt, Germany, the incidence of satanic activity among young people is widespread. After observing numerous teenage satanic dabblers during my high school assemblies, I was motivated with the help of a researcher to take one year off and investigate the occult movement—talk about a crash course in the bizarre! When I finished, I wrote about my findings in the book, *The Edge of Evil*. In some ways I wish that I didn't know as much about satanism as I do. I wish that my research had comforted me with evidence that suggested very little satanic activity in America, because what I discovered during that year is the frightening reality that satanism is thriving and has its grips on a growing number of teenagers. You may not be particularly worried about satanism, but you *should* be.

Satanists—people who worship Satan as their god—seek to obtain power to manipulate the world around them for their own gain. They call upon the powers of Satan in certain prescribed rituals. Satanists strongly oppose the Judeo-Christian tradition and adhere to a system of personal power. Many of their teachings are directly antithetical to the precepts found in the Bible.

Satanic suicide (taking one's life at the command of Satan), homicide, and ritualistic deviant behavior have been documented nationwide. I have personally visited death row and interviewed one teenager who had shot his parents in cold blood for Ezurate, a demon entity that, he claimed, lived within him. Perhaps you have read accounts of satanic violence committed by young people. One involved Tommy Sullivan, fourteen, who slashed his mother's throat, stabbed her several times, and tried to gouge her eyes out. Found later in a snowdrift near his home in Jefferson Township, New Jersey, with self-imposed lacerations on both wrists and neck, all that remains of Tommy are these words written in his own handwriting:

To the greatest of demons:

I would like to make a solemn exchange with you. If you will give me the most extreme of all magical powers, I will kill many Christian followers. Exactly twenty years from this day I promise to commit suicide. I will tempt teenagers on earth to have sex, have incest, do drugs, and worship you. I believe that evil will once again rise and conquer the love of God.

Teens at the edge of evil

For many of America's youth, satanism is simply something to dabble in. Similar to the curiosity and intrigue of a party seance or a Ouija board, satanism promises teens the inviting world of power, sex, and drugs. Many kids experiment with it for the thrill, never really believing in its power. They enter into the realm of the occult, having no idea that it is cleverly disguised self-destruction. Helping them to descend the dark ladder is occult literature like Anton LaVey's *Satanic Bible*, which has sold more than one million copies. Heavy-metal music, fantasy role games, and secretive covens all contribute to teens' becoming enslaved by satanism.

Criminologists, mental health therapists, clergy, psychiatrists, and counselors have heard the grisly stories about youthful involvement in satanic activity. The exact perimeters of the movement may never be known because secrecy is one of the characteristics of satanism. But satanic fascination among teens is growing. Visit any American high school and you will most likely notice at least a few students dressed totally in black with satanic symbols or insignia attached to their clothing or tattooed on their skin. The response from skeptics is that such attire is a fad—a deliberate attempt to shock adults. I don't buy that. These kids are being recruited, often against their own will and without their knowledge, into the dark and destructive world of evil.

And though in some circles it is not popular to admit this, I firmly believe that Satan is actively involved in dragging these kids into his kingdom.

A *literal devil?*

Many people scoff at the concept of a real, literal devil. Even some Christians have a hard time believing that Satan is a real entity. As far as I'm concerned, that's "hope-so theology." And it's dangerous! A careful study of the Bible reveals that next to God, there is no one more powerful than Satan. From his cunning deceit in the Garden of Eden to his brief "triumph" at Golgotha and continuing now in our century, Satan has been hard at work trying to destroy all that is good. What better target than a teenager, barely beyond the age of innocence but eager to try something new and exciting? The great British writer C. S. Lewis once stated that Satan's greatest work is to disguise his identity, and I heartily agree. While many in the church debate the existence of a literal devil, Satan is robbing the church of its youth. *We had better begin taking notice.*

Many kids get into satanism not realizing what they have bargained for. According to reports filed with police departments in towns and cities across the nation, one of the more popular recruitment techniques begins with an invitation to a party. Word goes out that there will be plenty of drugs, sex, and alcohol. After the kids are sufficiently under the influence of the drugs or alcohol, a few are invited into a private room that, they are told, only a select few may enter. Inside the room, other teens are involved in group sex, and it isn't long before the initiates join in. What they don't realize at the time, however, is that while they are participating, a hidden video camera is recording everything. As the sexual activity progresses, someone suggests that they invoke a contract or covenant with Satan to give them more power. Often, blood is spilled through a small cut and someone offers an initiation prayer to Lucifer (or one of his many names). The initiates think that this is the ultimate in a "theme party" and willingly participate. But later, after the party is over and they begin to have second thoughts about their actions, the pressure to continue with the group in other activities begins. And when they try to drop out, the videotape of their sexual exploits appears as blackmail.

Sounds farfetched? Unbelievable? I thought so, too, but this recruitment technique has been documented and taught to other police groups by veteran cop Jerry Simandl of the Chicago Police Department's Gang Crime Unit.

Remember: Deception is the hallmark of Satan. It is not uncommon for teens to be integrated into secretive covens without their initial knowledge. Coven leaders try to get kids involved in illegal behavior (using and selling drugs, production and distribution of pornography, prostitution) to further incriminate them and keep them within the coven. Testimonies of kids who were once involved in satanism but have defected reveal that initiates are monitored, followed, threatened, drugged, and psychologically tortured in order to be controlled.

No teen who is given a glimpse of the miserable path of satanism would ever start to dabble. But again, satanism is clever. It disguises self-destruction with things that seem so curious and entertaining. Once the trap closes, it's almost impossible to escape. Did you note how many of the letters at the beginning of this chapter even mentioned a desire to get out?

Protecting your teen from satanism

If I asked any parent if he or she would object to a son's or daughter's getting involved in satanic activity, I know what the answer would be: "Absolutely! I hope our child *never* falls for it." Yet I'm amazed at how blind we can be to the subtle influences of satanism around us. This is serious business. Many of the other problems mentioned in this book are so visible, but Satan seldom shows his face: His agenda may be hidden in any number of things that appear harmless. As a parent you need to be on your guard for his cunning work. With satanism, prevention is easier than deliverance.

Prevention begins at home by your teaching your teenager the truth about Satan. Impress upon your teen the power of evil. Remind your young person that any religion that focuses on destruction, deceit, and degradation *cannot* be good. At the same time, stress the ultimate power of God who has victory over Satan. Your goal is to teach your teenager to understand and respect the power of Satan but not to fear it. A young person with a firm commitment to God is less likely to fall for Satan's lies.

The Bible exhorts, "Do not give the devil a foothold," (Ephesians 4:27). The best way for you to accomplish that as a parent is to warn your kids about potential satanic involvement in occult literature, horror films, and extreme heavy-metal music. I am also convinced that some fantasy role-playing games can actually have satanic elements and tend to lead kids into a fascination with the occult. Sean Sellers, a former satanist now on death row for the murder of his parents, has made it clear that he was introduced to satanism through playing the popular game Dungeons and Dragons. Does this mean that Dungeons and Dragons is satanic? Not necessarily, but I have heard enough reports of kids entering satanism through this door to make me think that you need to become concerned if your kids seem obsessed with it. My hunch is that anything that has an almost magnetic pull on teens will be used by Satan. For example, an objective book describing satanism may in itself be fine, but for a teenager fascinated by the bizarre, it could ignite a burning desire to learn more—maybe even to experience Satan's power.

This is an important distinction, and it may help you explain to your teen how Satan works. The wrong approach is to tell your teen to quit wearing a certain T-shirt because "it's satanic." Your teen will probably scoff at the idea and dismiss you as some sort of paranoid fanatic. It's far better to tell your teen that a T-shirt by itself may not be satanic, but if it begins to create a compulsive fascination for more of the same, Satan may be using those things to gain a foothold.

I have found that kids from disruptive homes seem to be most vulnerable to satanism. I think that's because there is within all of us a yearning for orderliness and security—a sense of belonging to something bigger than ourselves. In my study of the superstructure of covens I have found that it is secretive, tight-knit, loyalist, and protective. There is a high priest and priestess, generally, at regular meetings. (This is true even if the coven is comprised of teen dabblers.) To the disillusioned teen, the coven represents a pseudo-family. Finally, he can belong. Obviously, that ought to encourage us to strengthen the family unit, reduce the chaos, establish regular patterns such as a shared family meal, family devotions, perhaps a family project. I cannot recall having met one teen who had left a genuine, caring family for a coven.

Building self-esteem in your teen will also help protect her from satanism. One of the initial attractions of the coven is the opportunity to be somebody. That's why role-playing games can become a natural avenue for moving into the occult. The insecure, withdrawn teenager can assume a brand-new identity. In some cases, the coven will give the new member a brand-new name. What a rush for someone who has not been affirmed by his family and friends! Be careful when you discipline that you do not berate your teen. Always try to find ways to accentuate the positive, to recognize your child's personhood. Self-knowledge and self-acceptance are great defenses against the deceitful promise of identity that comes with satanism.

Closely related to the identity that is promised by satanism is the appeal of being accepted by the group, regardless of who you are or what you look like. Satanic covens are best at this. They are the archetypal home for the rejected and forlorn: "If you're not good enough for any of the cliques in your high school, try our secret little group. There's room for you there." I think that this is a real indictment and yet a challenge to the church. I hope that your church has an active, dynamic youth group and that it is inclusive. I hope that no one feels that he's not popular enough or that she's not cool enough to belong to your church's youth group. I hope that your own son or daughter feels comfortable going to the youth activities in your church. If not, find out why. Belonging to a lively youth group is a tremendous deterrent to the appeal of the occult, and I'm troubled when I hear some of the rougher kids in high schools say that they feel that they would never be welcome in some church circles.

Hitting close to home

Okay, you're reading along and getting a sinking feeling in the pit of your stomach. Your teenager has been getting together with his friends a couple of nights a week to play a fantasy role-playing game. He has a couple of black T-shirts emblazoned with a skull and the name of a heavy-metal rock group. He's spending less time with his old friends and says that he doesn't want to go to church anymore. "Jerry," you ask frantically, "is he into satanism?"

Probably not. But you are wise to notice these signals. The scenario described above is not altogether unusual and it is most likely that your teen is more interested in shocking you than in worshiping the devil. I would describe this teen as dabbling—taking a peek into the dark and mysterious. If you will recall your own youth, you might remember having been drawn to that summertime ritual of listening to ghost stories around the campfire. Today there are too many graphic manifestations of scariness, so you must be on your guard.

If your son or daughter appears to be dabbling in the occult, make sure that the communication lines are open. Ask about his interest in the games and music. Have her explain how the game works or ask to see some of the lyrics of the music so that you can understand them better. Even if you are fearful, don't approach your teen with an attitude of fear. If it's a case of simple dabbling, chances are that your child will be a little embarrassed and may decide to dabble in something less weird. Your reaction may, in fact, be more important than you think. If your teen is trying to shock you and succeeds, she may try something a little more serious the next time. Don't give her a reason to play with fire.

If, however, you sense that your teen's dabbling is more serious, I advise counseling. It's serious if drug or alcohol use accompanies some of the other signals. Your teen's defenses are being neutralized—she's finding it harder to stay away from occult trappings. Needs aren't being met, hence there's a yearning to move further into darkness. Ask your pastor to recommend a psychologist for adolescents who is also a committed Christian, then make an appointment. And be wary of any believer (counselor, clergy, or layperson) who uses the language of "being demon-possessed." In my opinion, the majority of these kids who are even serious dabblers are *not* demon-possessed. They are troubled kids who need emotional, psychological, and spiritual guidance *before* they become hopelessly trapped in satanism.

Actually, you can take some wry comfort in seeing your teen visibly demonstrating an interest in the occult. Remember that satanism is a deceitful, secretive movement. True satanists generally are two-faced: normal, law-abiding citizens by day, robed coven members at night. Frankly, I worry more about those adult people than the misdirected kids who are dabbling in the occult. If we reach them when they're still pretending, we may save them from selling out to the Great Deceiver.

Teenage occult warning signs

- Withdrawal, alienation from family and friends
- New, small group of friends
- Wearing dark colors (black, dark purple)
- Collecting occult items or designs
- Comments about hearing voices
- Preoccupation with death, anarchy, destruction
- Excessive interest in fantasy role-playing games
- Avid interest in occult literature
- Aggressive, violent behavior
- Isolation, moodiness, depression
- Maintenance of a satanic diary, often called "book of shadows"
- Interest in heavy-metal music
- Excessive use of drugs or alcohol
- Signs of sexual promiscuity
- Evidence of self-mutilation

Occult paraphernalia
- Black robes; detachable hoods
- Incense, flash powder, smoke bombs
- Small velvet pillow, usually scarlet
- Chalice, goblet
- Body paint/face paint
- Sword, knives, daggers
- Candles, skull, or bone collection
- Books on satanism and magic
- Wooden stand or marble slab for altar
- Gongs, bells, drums, crosses

9

TEEN PREGNANCY

"I'm 13 years old and I'm pregnut."

DEAR JERRY,

At age 14 I lost my virginity. Not out of peer pressure but out of ignorance. I was naive and never knew or wondered what was right or wrong. Now I do, but it's too late. I've had sex with seven different guys. Two of them were virgins. I feel bad now that I invaded their virginity. One of them is my present boyfriend. We have had sex 21 times. Almost half the time we've used a condom. I need some advice.

LINDSAY

▼▼▼▼▼▼▼▼▼▼▼▼▼

DEAR JERRY,

I'm 13 years old and I'm pregnut. I was drunk and a guy took advantage of me. I use to do drugs and drink. I don't now because I want a healthy baby. I'm five months along but my dad won't let me keep the baby, and that is the most important thing to me. I don't know what to do. I'm so alone. I hate my dad for what he is doing to me. I want to get to see my baby, to hold it and love it. Please help me.

KATIE

▼▾▼▾▼▾▼▾▼▾▼▾▼▾

DEAR MR. JOHNSTON,

Two years ago I fell in love with Barry. He never loved me though. So I was determined to make him love me. I fell into a deep depression. I shut my family out and started failing in school. Then of course came alcohol and drugs. One night I was drunk and kind of out of it. I was screaming and crying at Barry to love me and he said, "Maybe someday." That night I lost my virginity at age 15. Now I feel so dirty.

KARMIN

▼▾▼▾▼▾▼▾▼▾▼▾▼▾

DEAR JERRY,

I have never drank, done drugs, or had sex. But I feel so much pressure from my friends to do these things. Usually when you say everyone is doing it you think everyone really isn't. But I swear, when it comes to sex everyone is doing it! I just went to my friend's party. Alcohol was everywhere, and people were having sex right there on the floor. One of my friends came up to me and said, "Tiffany, I have finally found a way to forget everything: sex and alcohol." She was a virgin until that night. She got laid by ten guys that night.

TIFFANY

▼▾▼▾▼▾▼▾▼▾▼▾▼▾

DEAR JERRY,

Last year in the eighth grade I got mixed up in the wrong crowd. I tried speed twice. Then I started skipping school with my friends. One day when I skipped I went off with this guy and lost my virginity to him. He wasn't anything special.

AMBER

▼▼▼▼▼▼▼▼▼▼▼▼▼

DEAR MR. JOHNSTON,

As a high school senior I was looking forward to graduation. The kids at school have always teased me for being so straight. I began the school year being the only virgin in my class, as far as I know. I guess I got discouraged and fell into the trap of wanting to be like everyone else. Slowly, I can't explain why. I began giving in to my boyfriend's sexual demands. Now I wish I had never met this guy. Being like everyone else isn't what I thought it would be. The kids still tease me because they think I'm still a virgin. That just makes me feel worse.

MARY KAY

▼▼▼▼▼▼▼▼▼▼▼▼▼

DEAR JERRY,

Everyone at school hates me. I think that if I wasn't a virgin I would have more friends. I don't fit in. Almost all the girls in my school have had sex. Many of them have gotten pregnant. Some have had abortions and some kept their babies. I want a baby so bad Jerry. A baby would put some joy into my life. Nothing else seems to be working.

CARRIE

▼▼▼▼▼▼▼▼▼▼▼▼▼

117

DEAR JERRY,

I am 14 years old and I'm still a virgin. I want to save myself for the husband I will find someday, but I am feeling a lot of pressure to give in. I almost lost my virginity a year and a half ago. I backed away at the last minute. There is really no one I can talk to about my feelings.

JOY

JERRY,

I had sex so many times before the sixth grade that I can't even remember all my partners. During the ninth grade I had seventy-six sexual encounters. I know that sounds ridiculous, but I did it. In high school, I got into lots of trouble. Of course, the fact that I had sex with three of my teachers didn't help. I'm really scared. I feel so much guilt, shame, anger, and failure.

SHARON

DEAR JERRY,

My life really started going downhill in the seventh grade when my father died. I started having a lot of family problems. I really messed up bad. Here I am 14 years old and pregnant. Just what I really needed. You always think it will never happen to me, but it did.

MICHELLE

DEAR JERRY,

I have slept with 16 guys. I've been laid 98 times. I guess that makes me a slut. In the last year I've thought of suicide constantly. As of now it's been a month and a half since my last sexual encounter. I hope it stays that way.

ROBIN

▼▼▼▼▼▼▼▼▼▼▼▼▼

DEAR MR. JOHNSTON,

The other day in school a guy in my class had a T-shirt on that said, "I'm Not Doin' It!" It was refering to sex. One guy made fun of him for wearing it, so I defended the guy with the shirt. Suddenly the whole class was listening.

HUTCH

▼▼▼▼▼▼▼▼▼▼▼▼

When I read thirteen-year-old Katie's letter, I couldn't help but notice the irony. Katie knew how to have sex but couldn't even spell the results of her sexuality. Like many other teenagers, she understands the mechanics of sexual intercourse but is totally unprepared to deal with the emotional, social, and spiritual consequences of "making love." In most cases, these kids aren't making anything but babies.

So it goes with more than eleven million sexually active teens. Encouraged by a sexually explicit environment, they have sex but are left with all the baggage that comes with promiscuity: guilt, pregnancy, disease, premature marriage, and low self-esteem. Surgeon General Antonia Novello warns that more than two-thirds of U.S. adolescents will be sexually active before they leave high school. By age eighteen more than 60% of the guys and almost half the girls will have experienced sexual intercourse. Says Surgeon General Novello, "The estimated average age for first intercourse is sixteen to twenty in some urban areas. More than 20% of high school students have had four or more partners. Anal intercourse—a likely HIV infection risk factor—may involve 10% to 26% of all sexually active adolescents."

Consider some of the findings of an extensive survey conducted by *Seventeen* magazine, the magazine of choice for middle and upper-middle class teenage girls:

- Only 21% of the girls and 15% of the guys think that premarital sex is a bad idea for everyone.
- In 1984, 54% of girls ages 18 to 19 had sex; in 1991 that number has jumped to 71%.
- Six out of ten sexually active teens worry about getting AIDS.
- Of those who've had sex, the average age for first intercourse is 15.8.

The results of these attitudes are predictable. The Children's Defense Fund reports that 2,700 teens a day become pregnant, most unintentionally. Contrary to popular opinion, pregnant teens are not just the poor or urban girls; 61% of all teen mothers are white. Contraceptives are used by only 23% of teens fifteen and under, the first month they have sex. After a year of sexual activity, 42% did not use contraceptives. Of the one million unwed girls who become pregnant each year, almost half of them terminate their pregnancies through abortion.

When I cite these findings about teenage sexual promiscuity, Christian parents will often remind me that this kind of information applies only to kids from unchurched homes. "Thank the Lord, *our* kids aren't like that," they say. Well, as kids respond these days, "Not!" According to youth expert Josh McDowell and separate polls by George Gallup Jr. and the Presbyterian Church,

church kids are only slightly behind their secular counterparts in terms of their sexual activity. According to McDowell's extensive survey of churched youth, 40% have had sexual intercourse by age eighteen. By age thirteen, 20% of the churched youth had participated in some form of sexual experimentation. *We can no longer assume that just because we take our kids to church and send them to their youth groups that they will postpone sexual activity.* According to practically every reliable indicator, if you have a sixteen-year-old you can be reasonably sure that he or she has engaged in some form of sexual activity. You can be *absolutely* certain that your teen has been regularly tempted and, in some cases, pressured to engage in inappropriate sexual behavior.

Whom to blame

All you have to do is open your eyes and look at the cultural landscape if you want to understand why your teenager may have problems with remaining a virgin. Practically every product aimed at the teen market— clothes, shoes, candy, gum, soda pop, beer, music, makeup, even deodorant—is promoted heavily with strong sexual innuendo. Have you watched much prime time television lately? Last year the big theme for every sitcom and drama was "time to quit being a virgin." This was with teen characters like Doogie Howser! Each show outdid itself trying to make it seem "meaningful" or the result of much moral introspection. But the message was always the same: "Sex is okay when you're a teenager as long as you practice safe sex and think highly of your partner." And if your kids aren't quite sure how to go about "doing it," they can walk into a corner store and buy pornography; or easier still, attend any R-rated movie that contains erotic scenes of men and women making love.

At least the advertisers are somewhat subtle in their use of sex to sell shoes to kids. The music industry is so blatant that it's almost embarrassing to read the lyrics of popular songs. Do you have any idea what happens to the already revved-up hormones of a fourteen-year-old when she hears the words, "I wanna sex you up," over and over again in her earphones. But that's what Color Me Badd, extremely popular with teen and preteen girls, sings to your daughter. And those lyrics are tame compared to the offerings from other groups!

But music, movies, and advertising are the *easy* targets. For many of us they become the scapegoat—almost an excuse for letting our kids do things that we know are wrong. So let's look at another factor that may be sending our kids the message that teen premarital sex is okay: parents. I know that sounds harsh, but before you take issue with me, ask yourself this question: When was the last time I sat down and talked with my children about sex? Numerous teens have told me that they *never* learned anything about sex from their parents. The vast majority of teens get their information about sex from their peers (talk about the blind leading the blind!). That's why 93% of the nation's high schools offer some form of sex education. They *have* to, because no one else is doing it. Not parents, not the church, no one!

Consider this scenario: Thirteen-year-old Julie went to a party at a friend's house. It was chaperoned by her friend's parents, and no alcohol was served. Tom, a boy whom Julie liked, sat next to her all evening and eventually put his arm around her. Later, they all watched a movie, *Porky's*, and in the darkened room, Tom slipped his hand onto Julie's breast. She wanted to push it away but decided not to. That's as far as anything went, but Julie felt pretty bad and confused at the same time. At a sleep-over the next weekend, she talked about it with her friend Tammy. When she described what had happened,

Tammy responded, "Cool, that must have been great!" When Julie admitted that she felt kind of guilty about letting Tom touch her that way, Tammy just laughed and said, "Wait until he gets under your bra. You won't feel so bad then!"

How much better it would have been if Julie had been able to go and share her confusion with her mother. But Mom was always too busy to talk during the day and too tired to listen at night. So Julie's values about her own sexuality are being shaped by her thirteen-year-old friend who has already made up her mind that sex is cool.

Sure, we live in a day when sex has been devalued by our culture. And I agree that it's hard to raise chaste kids when so much of popular media encourage young people to become sexually active. But that doesn't mean that we should abdicate our responsibility as parents. The best sex education is that which occurs in the home. Reed Larsen, professor of human development at the University of Illinois points out, however, that in the period between ages ten and fifteen, the amount of time that young people spend with their families decreases by half. That's the time when we ought to be spending *more* time instilling moral values in our children.

Helping your teen stay chaste

Someone once told me that sex on the first date for today's teen is the equivalent to getting a kiss on the first date when I was a teen. I don't know if it's really that bad, but all the indicators suggest that kids are having sex earlier and more frequently than ever before. The world that your sons or daughters live in expects them to become sexually active while still in their teens. What can you do about it?

You can begin by talking about sex frankly and honestly. That sounds easy, but if you have not talked with your child about sex when she was four or five, you will find that it's even harder to talk about it with a teenager. But talk you must. Your teen needs to know that it's okay for him to talk with you about sex. If he thinks you can't handle it, he will rely on what he's learning in the locker room. I will go so far as to say if you do not talk honestly with your teen about sex, you can almost be certain that your son or daughter will be more likely to engage in sexual intercourse before marriage and while still a teen living at home. Count on it!

Don't just *talk* about sex; *listen.* Ask direct questions: Is Tom putting pressure on you to have sex? Do you think that Tina is trying to tell you something when she dresses the way that she does? Ask him how he deals with his own desires. Ask her if she ever worries about whether or not her boyfriend may have had sex with others. Don't assume that your child knows everything about sex. Even though anatomically mature enough to engage in intercourse, your teenager may not really know how a woman becomes pregnant or how venereal disease is spread. You wouldn't believe some of the myths surrounding these issues: You can't get pregnant if you "do it" standing up; plastic wrap makes a good condom substitute; venereal disease will not spread through oral sex; withdrawal before ejaculation is a foolproof form of birth control. At first your teen will seem embarrassed to talk with you about these things, especially if you have not made sex a part of in-home education from an early age. But once he trusts you—sees that you aren't fazed by some of the slang expressions for anatomy—your young person will open up remarkably. Who wouldn't? Sex is a great subject; wonderfully interesting. Most teens would give anything to be able to discuss it freely with their parents.

As you talk with your teen about sex, always emphasize the importance of saving sexual intercourse for marriage. He will expect you to say this, but say it anyway. He needs to hear it, to be reassured that *someone* in this world believes in premarital chastity. Teens live with the impression that everybody's doing it and nobody cares. That may even frighten them, so your gentle reminder may give them the will to fight the trend. You may want to make a covenant with them. "If you promise to save sex for marriage, I promise to answer any question you have about sex anytime." Or something like that. Get your teenager to share as part of a team—Mom, Dad, and me—all aiming for the same worthy goal.

I don't think that it's healthy or helpful to impose a laundry list of rules on teens, but I believe that we do our kids a disservice if we don't guide them into behavior patterns that will help them remain chaste. Sometimes, a rule gives a teen a face-saving excuse for not going along with the crowd. A daughter who may be worried about giving in to pressure from a boyfriend will appreciate being able to say, "I can't come over to your house while your folks aren't home. My parents won't let me." I recommend a few well-defined rules regarding places to go and activities for dating teens. For example, a teen should not be allowed to be alone in a home with a girlfriend or boyfriend. So many of the sexually active kids I talk to say that they frequently have sex in their own homes. This is most prevalent in single-parent homes where there's a lag time of two to three hours between the end of school and the time that the parent gets home from work. I also think that it's wise to encourage double-dating and to set curfews. I know that rules regarding clothing seem parochial to some (and they are hard to enforce), but parents of teenage girls would be wise to try to limit extremely revealing bathing suits and other clothes that might attract undue attention from the guys. I do not buy the argument that a girl wearing a tight dress is "asking for it," but I do know that some guys need little encouragement. Better to err on the side of modesty.

The topic of sex gives us such a wonderful opportunity to talk to our kids about God, and this, too, can help them develop proper values and attitudes. Did you notice how many letters at the beginning of this chapter mentioned exact numbers regarding sexual intercourse? The writers had kept a record of each time they had engaged in sex. That only confirms what the Bible teaches—that there is something very special about sex. Never take the approach that sex is dirty or bad. Show your teen how God gave us sexuality as a gift—that it is something beautiful and lovely when it is enjoyed in the context of marriage. Read Song of Solomon together, telling your teen that it is, in essence, a sex manual of marital bliss. Help your son or daughter to see that God has already reserved a special person just for each of them and how wonderful it will be to make love with that person, with a completely clean conscience.

Your relationship with your spouse can also help your teen decide to save sex until marriage. In another chapter I mentioned the importance of showing affection to your spouse. Kids think that sex is something that only kids want to do; that once you get married you won't have any more fun. We reinforce that myth if we save all our cuddling, hugging, and kissing for the bedroom. Within the boundaries of good taste, let your kids see that the flame doesn't go out when the honeymoon is over.

Sexual healing

Since 50% of today's teens are having sex, there's a fair chance that your teen may no longer be a virgin. So what do you do if you learn that your teen has been sleeping with someone else? Is there anything you *can* do? I believe there is. In fact, I believe it's possible to help a sexually active teen return to abstinence, but realistically, that's a very rare occurrence. A teen who has been sexually active will struggle with trying to abstain, in most cases, all the ensuing time up into the marriage. In fact, some research suggests that premarital sex predisposes adults to be adulterous. Clearly, the sexually active teen will have a hard time turning from his or her past.

Even before you make any attempt to encourage a return to abstinence, I recommend testing for venereal disease. Some forms of syphilis and gonorrhea are making a comeback, and there is always the strong possibility of contracting AIDS through heterosexual contact, especially if one partner has been promiscuous. A side benefit to the test is something of a reality check for the teen. The very thought of carrying a life-threatening disease may help a teen reconsider his or her sexual activity. But in terms of public health, kids who are sexually active need to know if they have been infected.

You may need to do some serious soul-searching of your own. Do you *really* have strong convictions against premarital sex? Are you up to the task of helping your teen choose abstinence? If not, you may be wasting your time trying to promote something that you don't believe in or are unwilling to support with loving guidance. It would be better for you to acknowledge your teen's desire to be sexually active, and to spend your time and energy promoting birth control and protection from disease. I'm not being facetious, because I know there are many Christian parents who have thrown up their hands and let their kids live as they please. Don't do this. If the only influence you can exert is in the area of birth control and so-called "safe sex," take that opportunity and build on it. It may keep enough dialogue going to allow you to lead them back gradually toward abstinence.

The return to abstinence will be an uphill path, but it's not impassible. The first step is to get your teen to commit to it. Most likely, their own guilt will lead them to such a commitment, but guilt alone is never a good motivator. Follow up with some guidelines that will keep your teen away from temptation. Set goals and reward them when they succeed. Counseling may be helpful, especially if you can pair your teen up with a respected young adult who is committed to Christ and is a trained counselor. But sometimes, a youth pastor or even a grandparent can listen and encourage. Again the goal is to show your teen that you aren't the only one who believes in abstinence. One word of warning, however: Protect your teen's privacy. Do not force your teen to share this personal side of his life. The decision to seek counseling must be your teen's.

Finally, support your teen on your knees and communicate that you are praying for her daily. This is such a powerful resource, but so often we neglect to uphold our kids in our prayers. Pray specifically that God will heal the guilt that generally accompanies early sexual activity. Pray for supernatural strength for your teen. Pray for wisdom and patience as you seek to guide your teen back to abstinence.

I'm convinced that the subject of sex can bring us closer to our teens than can practically any other subject. It's such a powerful drive in their lives, and I believe that they want to talk with us about it. Let your teen know that you're ready to listen.

10

RAPE

"At the age of 13 I was raped."

DEAR JERRY,

A boy I used to date raped me. He took me off my school campus and we went to his house. I had broken up with him about a year ago so I could date the boy I date now. I guess ever since then he has been thinking of a way to get back at me. What he did has put me through hell. I have bad nightmares about him. I'm scared to death of him.

JULIA

DEAR JERRY,

I was raped by an ex-boyfriend last year and now I'm facing the decision of an abortion. I don't know what to do and what is right anymore. I don't want this baby. I don't want to look at it every day and see my ex-boyfriend's face. I know it's not right to kill my baby. Please write me back soon and help me.

DENISE

▼▼▼▼▼▼▼▼▼▼▼▼▼

DEAR JERRY,

I'm 14 and in the eighth grade. There is a girl at school I have known for two years and we have become good friends. But I don't know what to say to her anymore. She's only 13 and her dad raped her last year. She tried to kill herself so they put her in a hospital all summer and no one could get in touch with her. She got out of the hospital a week before school started, then she tried to kill herself again. I need to know what to do to help her.

SHARI

▼▼▼▼▼▼▼▼▼▼▼▼▼

JERRY,

At age 13 I was molested until I was about 16 by six men: my stepdad, an eye doctor, my godfather, a friend of my stepdad, a neighbor, and a stranger. I have been placed in several foster homes and I even went to a hospital. I am a very good volleyball player. That's what I like to do. Please do me this one favor and write me back.

BRANDIE

▼▼▼▼▼▼▼▼▼▼▼▼▼

DEAR JERRY,

At six years old I lost my virginity to a cousin. At 11 my new stepfather tried to molest me. At 12 I was raped by a perfect stranger. He happened to be black so my father calls me a "nigger lover." After this I decided life was a waste. I was having sex with anybody. I just didn't care anymore. At 13 I got pregnant by my 14 year-old boyfriend. At 16 I moved in with my 25 year-old boyfriend. I'm 17, soon to turn 18. I feel old, tired, depressed, and ready to give up.

CAROLYN

▼▼▼▼▼▼▼▼▼▼▼▼▼

DEAR JERRY,

At the age of 13 I was raped. It was on my thirteenth birthday. I turned to drugs, but because of the drugs I failed high school. I'm scared to live because I don't want to hurt or be lonely or feel trapped anymore.

SARAH

▼▼▼▼▼▼▼▼▼▼▼▼▼

DEAR JERRY,

This guy I used to date raped me. But I'm doing better now. The guy is in jail and I will be in court sometime. He'll get what he deserves. My mom transferred me to another school because the kids at my old school found out I had been raped and started talking bad to me. I couldn't handle that. It hurt me. Well, I'm excited about going to my new school. Thanks for all your help.

PAMELA

▼▼▼▼▼▼▼▼▼▼▼▼▼

DEAR JERRY,

I don't do drugs or drink or party. My family is well off. The day before my sixteenth birthday I went out.

There were three girls and three guys but I only knew one of the girls. It was my first time to drink. But one of the guys raped me. No one was around and it was my first time. I didn't want anyone to know. I felt so guilty! But I told a friend and she started telling people about it. Now everyone at school knows everything. I'm an outcast!

LISA

▼▼▼▼▼▼▼▼▼▼▼▼

DEAR MR. JOHNSTON,

When I was little my half-brother raped me. I never told anyone because I just couldn't face it. I'm sorry I had to bother you with this, but I didn't know who else to tell. I don't want to speak to my parents about it because my dad would only yell at me and my mom would say, "Well, there's nothing we can do now." I don't like to talk to adults.

KAY

▼▼▼▼▼▼▼▼▼▼▼▼

Nothing is sadder than listening to a teenager tell you that she has been raped. Many kids never tell their parents, and most rapes involving teenagers never get reported. Most of the victims suffer in silence. They are ashamed, afraid, and angry. And they are wary. They read the papers. They know that one of the first things that a girl must do is to prove that she didn't "ask for it." Even when victims endure the pain of a trial, the accused often goes free. Why bother?

I have never been able to understand the crime of rape. How could anyone force himself sexually against an unwilling victim? How could anyone do this to his own family member? And when rape involves a minor, I have a very difficult time containing my anger. Something is drastically wrong in our culture when young girls (and in some cases boys) are at risk of being raped.

Rape statistics are hard to come by and harder to believe. Officially, there were 91,000 rapes reported in the United States in 1990. Of those, some experts estimate as many as 10% may have involved minors. But since adult women in general and young women in particular are reluctant to report a rape, the total number of teenagers being raped could be much higher. Compounding the tragedy is that the number of reported rapes appears to be increasing.

For teenagers, so-called "date rape" is perhaps more of a problem than rape involving a complete stranger. Date rape is a term used to describe forced sex that occurs on a date. A guy will pressure his girlfriend to have sex and when she refuses he will physically force her to have sexual intercourse. The victim of a date rape finds herself in an extremely difficult situation. She may have genuinely liked the guy and wonders if it would be right to report the incident. She may be confused, wondering if maybe she did lead him on. She will most likely be frightened, especially if he tells her, "No one will believe you anyway, so just forget about it." As in any rape, she will feel "dirty" and ashamed. To tell someone seems like just so much more trauma. Consequently, most date rapes never get reported.

Rape prevention for teens

Isn't it a shame that we have to consider talking not just to young women but to females of every age nowadays about rape? I wish it weren't necessary, but it is. Sometime between the "birds and bees" talk and the onset of puberty, you would be wise to make sure that your daughter understands what rape is and how to protect herself from being raped. Generally, this is best done by

Mom, but it doesn't hurt to have both parents present. There are a number of organizations (including the local police department) who can provide you with helpful printed information.

Make sure that you cover the basic issues of where not to go and what not to do:

- avoid remote areas of parks and vacant lots, especially at night;
- never enter your car alone without checking the back seat;
- try not to leave a mall and head to the parking lot alone at night;
- don't jog, walk, or ride a bike alone at night;
- avoid situations in which you are outnumbered by a group of guys even if you know them.

These may seem like obvious suggestions, but don't assume that your daughter has been taught them.

Since most teen rapes involve a boyfriend or acquaintance, spend some time talking with your daughter about sexual pressure and harassment. I personally consider it rape if a boyfriend presses for sex until the girl gives in out of a sense of duty or just to "get it over with." That's not sex, that's rape. Tell your daughter that she never has to have sex unless it is *her* decision to have it (and stress marriage as the only proper modality for sex). I think it's also wise to warn your daughter about consenting to go with her boyfriend to any setting that is remote or secluded. Unless she completely trusts the guy, she could be placing herself in danger of rape.

One of the best ways for your daughter to protect herself from date rape is to double date. More and more I am seeing the value of double dates and "group dates," and I think that kids ultimately have a better time on these occasions. I realize that this flies in the face of current practice, and I know that this doesn't always go down well with our kids. But having a girlfriend along with her date can be awfully reassuring for both girls.

What I have to say next will surely sound like a dad talking, but it's an important consideration in any discussion of date rape. Dads, know whom your daughter is dating. Insist on meeting the young man. Without being intimidating, look him squarely in the eye, shake his hand, talk to him for a few minutes. Be friendly; try to establish some common ground. I can't prove this, but I have a hunch that any guy even remotely considering taking advantage of a girl will think twice if he has met the father and talked with him before dating his daughter.

How should you advise your daughter on the issue of self-defense? This is a very tough question and there are two schools of thought. Some advise women to fight, scream, claw, kick, and do everything to run away from an attacker. Others say that the best thing to do is remain passive. I really don't know what is best, but it is something you need to think through and talk with your daughter about. You know your daughter best—her psychological makeup, her physical strength, etcetera. If a girl is somewhat aggressive physically and responds well under stress, she might be able to escape an attack. But many law enforcement personnel (and convicted rapists) say that the struggle can intensify the rapist's desire and place the girl in greater danger of being seriously injured or killed. Conversely, when a victim remains passive, she may have a tendency to feel even more than normal guilt. They may always second-guess themselves, feeling that they could have prevented this awful occurrence.

As you can see, this is almost an impossible call. I tend to lean more toward advising any girl or woman to remain passive and pray. I once heard about a woman who was attacked and who began repeating the name of

Jesus as her clothes were being ripped from her body. As she continued repeating our Lord's name, the man stopped, apologized, then fled. Obviously, we can't count on that to happen every time, but I believe that a woman has a better chance of staying alive if she does not fight back. If you decide to encourage your daughter to fight back, I highly advise you to enroll her in self-defense classes. Check with your local YMCA or YWCA.

Incest: the unmentionable crime

You may have noticed that a large number of letters referred to rape by a relative or family member. This has to be one of the worst crimes against a human being. If proof of the utter depravity of man is ever needed, the crime of incest provides the evidence.

What makes incest so insidious is that it is so unnatural to be suspicious of a family member. There is a built-in level of trust between relatives that gives children a profound sense of security. They may be frightened of strangers, but who would suspect an uncle or father to hurt them? Then when it happens, their world is shattered. They feel confusion, shame, anger, and fear all at once. No wonder that so many of the kids I've talked with who have been incest victims want to kill themselves.

No parent wants to talk to a son or daughter about incest, but it is vitally important that your kids know that it is inappropriate for a family member to touch them sexually. They should also know that if a brother or other relative is bothering them, they should let you know. So many victims have said that their parents either brushed them off or expressed outrage that they would make such an accusation. Parents, listen to your child if he or she tries to talk to you about an embarrassing incident with a relative. Be alert to changes in behavior such as a sudden avoidance of a favorite relative. Don't be afraid to take the initiative with a question such as, "Does the way Uncle Fred holds you on his lap make you uncomfortable?" It might show them that they can confide in you and it might prevent something more serious from happening.

Finally, if your teen has been victimized by incest, do not try to ignore the problem. Often, parents are either too embarrassed or simply too distraught to address the problem. Seek professional counseling immediately for your teen. Report the offense to police authorities. Stand by your teen through every step of the journey toward healing.

Healing the pain of rape

I cannot imagine receiving a phone call late at night from a sobbing daughter crying, "Daddy, I've been raped!" My heart goes out to any parent who answers that call. Hearing the news is bad enough, but what may be even more difficult is the fact that how you respond can directly affect the healing process. Emotional trauma often impairs our judgment, and few things could be more traumatic than hearing that your daughter has been raped or sexually abused. What your daughter will need most is love and acceptance. She does not need to see your anger, nor does she need to be reminded that she shouldn't have been out by herself at night. Your very first words to her should be, "Honey, I love you and I'm so sorry that this happened." The hows and whys will be answered later. All you need to do at this point is wrap her in your love.

Explain to your daughter that the rape must be reported to the police and that she should be seen by a physician. If possible, call your hospital emergency room and explain that your daughter has been raped and that you would like to have her examined and treated. Then call the police and ask them to have a female detective meet you at the hospital to obtain information about the rape. Police agencies have become much more sensitive to the crime of rape and will make sure that your daughter is questioned politely by a female officer if at all possible. Even at this early stage in recovery your daughter needs to see that she has the power to help herself. Answering a detective's questions, describing her assailant, even allowing the physician to examine her—all contribute to her eventual moving from being a victim to being an overcomer. This is important to the healing process.

The police and/or hospital will no doubt have a crisis counselor available immediately to help your daughter through the initial trauma. Beyond that, your daughter will need additional counseling. Your pastor or school counselor can recommend counselors who are trained especially for this. Tragically, the biggest emotional problem that rape victims experience is guilt. Counseling will help alleviate those feelings, but you can assist by letting your daughter know that what happened was not her fault.

Spiritual guidance can also help a rape victim, but go easy on the "preaching." Point your daughter to verses dealing with God's unconditional love (Ephesians 3:18; 1 John 3:1). Read, with her, passages that speak of safety, comfort, compassion (Psalm 23; Psalm 31:1–5; Matthew 5:3–12; 2 Corinthians 2:4). Encourage your daughter to pray when she is afraid, cry out to God when she is angry. Let her know that you pray for her daily.

If there is any redeeming aspect of rape, it is the same that comes in any tragedy. The victim understands the pain of this crime better than anyone else and can help others who have been similarly violated. In light of this, encourage your daughter to volunteer her services to agencies that deal with rape victims. It may be something as "simple" as taking calls at a telephone hotline for rape victims. Whatever the effort, helping someone else through the trauma will further erase the guilt and give your daughter a tremendous psychological boost. It will also help someone else survive.

A word to our sons

Is your son a potential rapist? What a horrible thought, but it's possible. Without blaming society or culture, take a look at his world. At a time when his hormones are raging, he is surrounded by images of sexual license. The blatant message from those images is that he deserves to have sex. It's every man's right to do it whenever and with whomever he wants. If he watches prime-time television or attends movies, he sees forced sex glorified and romanticized. If he has ever seen a pornographic magazine or movie, he has probably been introduced to the sick idea that raping a woman is sexually gratifying to both rapist and victim. He may be a good kid, get decent grades, attend church every Sunday, but if he has assimilated the message that "women want it," he could be the perpetrator of a date rape.

If you do nothing else on this issue, at least sit down and explain that date rape will be treated as rape in a court of law and that it *is* a felony. Warn your son that pressuring a girl to do anything sexually against her will could lead to a charge of rape. Tell him that if he attempts to have sex and his date says no—but after repeated attempts she finally gives in, he could be arrested the next day on a rape charge. I firmly believe that if more fathers explained this to their sons, the number of date rapes would be cut in half. Have you had this conversation with your son yet?

Naturally, the best way to prevent your son from a rape charge is to teach him the truth about sexuality and relationships between men and women. As a parent you can help him see through the myths that distort a man's view of women. You can teach him to treat every girl with respect. You can also help him to respect himself. No "real

139

man" would harm a woman in any way. There is nothing macho about abusing a girl. The strongest men are those who can be kind, gentle, and protective of a woman. Fathers need to model this for their sons every day. Remember, your son is picking up one message from culture. Will he get a different one at home?

It is a shame that sex has become increasingly linked with violence. I fear that a generation of young men are developing a warped view of sex and that the corresponding generation of young women are becoming resigned to the idea that they were meant to be the property of some guy. This is happening in a supposedly liberated, sexually free society. All that this says to me is that we have strayed far from the biblical design of sex. I challenge you to join me in bucking the trend. Sex education belongs in the home. It should begin in the primary years and continue until our children are married (and maybe *after* they are married!). The world has brought sex out in the open, but for many Christians it's still a taboo subject. Let's not allow the world to set the agenda. Take advantage of the openness and teach your children the beauty and purity of sex as God designed it.

11

MENTAL / EMOTIONAL ILLNESS

"I have been mentally disturbed."

DEAR JERRY,

> I have not been into drugs or alcohol, but I have been mentally disturbed. I was in a mental hospital in July. I was there five weeks. The reason I'm writing is that I'm lonely. I went to a church youth group tonight and everyone made faces at me and laughed at me. I feel like a reject. What should I do?
>
> KAREN

DEAR JERRY,

> You seem like a real caring person and I thought you would understand if I told you I have been thinking

141

about killing myself. I have never tried it before but ever since I have been locked up in treatment centers I see no reason to live. I don't need to be locked up just for somebody to listen and understand me instead of yelling at me. I am 14.

JODIE

DEAR JERRY,

Last February my school found out that I wanted to commit suicide. The had my parents take me to a psychologist. I ended up in an institute of neuropsychiatry. I was there for four months off and on. I am presently taking medication so I don't hear voices and I'm also taking anti-depressants. At the present I am still locked up. I hate it here and I want to go home.

CLAUDIA

DEAR MR. JOHNSTON,

I am presently in a mental ward at a hospital. I hate being away from my friends and loved ones. I feel like the hospital makes me more depressed although I am trying to be more positive. I miss home. I hate this place. It makes me angry at the world. I am 16 and a cheerleader at my high school. I'm just your ordinary teenager who's confused about life and the future. Help.

DONNA

JERRY,

I am writing from a group home because I need 24-hour supervision. I hallucinate, and it's scary. I take medication that seems to make me feel like dying all the time. I'm 16.

COLLEEN

▼▼▼▼▼▼▼▼▼▼▼▼▼

DEAR JERRY,

As I am writing you I'm sitting in a hospital for teens who are in depression. I'm here because I was going to commit suicide. I hated the way I looked and acted. It just seemed as if I did not have anything to live for. I was lucky my Mom noticed I was sinking into depression.

BEN

▼▼▼▼▼▼▼▼▼▼▼▼▼

DEAR JERRY,

I have been in three psychiatric hospitals and have seen a number of therapists. For the past six or seven years I've just spiraled downward. I thought it would be fitting to take my life on the day I was born. Please let Jerry himself read this.

ALICE

▼▼▼▼▼▼▼▼▼▼▼▼▼

The letters I get from teenagers who have been in mental hospitals or have experienced severe psychological problems are especially touching. So often they feel as if no one cares. What's happening to our kids? Why are we seeing so many of our teenagers in therapy?

Mental illness is nothing to ignore, nor is it something to be ashamed of. It is, I'm convinced, a by-product of the type of culture that surrounds us. Until we see a return to more traditional values in our society, the problem of mental illness will only increase. Kids cannot be exposed to the steady diet of sex, alcohol, violence, drugs, degrading music, divorce, and two-faced adults without going crazy . . . literally. If we really knew what goes on in an average teen's home, what his friends do when no one's around, what it's like to violate your own conscience out of fear for your life, we might better understand why so many teens need professional psychiatric intervention. They have reached the limit and cannot go on anymore.

The avoidance trap

Too many times a parent refuses to admit the obvious when a child displays evidence of mental illness. Part of that lies in an unfortunate stigma attached to this condition, and part of it is due to pride. We just don't want to admit that our kids could have such problems.

When this happens, the problem will only get worse. What could be handled with a few counseling sessions as an outpatient turns into the nightmare of responding to traumatic behavior. I can't emphasize enough the importance of seeking professional help the moment you notice signals of mental or psychological instability (see chapter 13, "Kids on the Edge: Warning Signals").

If you or your spouse are hesitant to take that step, talk with your pastor or school counselor about your fears. They will be able to show you that you aren't the only parent who's had to seek such help, and they can also settle your mind about the nature of mental illness. The image of a catatonic zombie being hauled away in a straightjacket to a padded cell is a relic of the past. Like other groups in medicine, the mental health profession has discovered new methods of treatment and understands the importance of compassionate, dignified care. It would be a shame if you avoided such care simply because you are embarrassed or fearful.

As you become confident of the help that is available, you may need to convince your teen that such a step will give him relief from his problems. There might be resistance at first: "I don't need a shrink!" Explain that from time to time we all need help with our problems and that today there are many more resources available than in the past. Focus on words such as *rest, relief, comfort, safe, private.* The teen is being squeezed from many directions and will surely resonate with anything that sounds non-threatening.

An ounce of prevention

Of course, no one plans to spend time in a mental hospital. Those who need the services of a psychiatrist have gotten to that point because they haven't developed healthy ways to cope with the stress and pressure in their lives. Most have a very low self-esteem. They do not like the way they look or act. They feel inferior.

Make sure that you create the kind of environment in your home that minimizes the potential for severe psychological problems in your teen. Please consult my "Twenty Prescriptions for Effective Communication with Teenagers" and make sure that you are employing these regularly. It's so important that you keep the lines of communication open between you and your teenager. This will help you spot problems before they become serious.

Be very discerning when it comes to self-esteem problems. I believe that more kids eventually need psychiatric care because of low self-esteem than because of any other problem. It seems to be the core need for so many teen problems such as drug and alcohol abuse, the occult, or suicide. Sometimes we mistake our teen's swagger as conceit when it actually is an attempt to hide her fear. Deep down inside she is not pleased with who she is. As a general rule, I recommend that parents err on the side of heaping too much rather than too little praise on their kids. Build them up constantly. Make them feel like somebody. Focus on those things they do well and stroke their egos. Even when you have to discipline them, *never* berate or put down. This is dangerous if there is even a slight problem of low self-esteem. When a teen is convinced that her parent has given up on her, she concludes that there's no hope.

I'm also a firm believer in old-fashioned things like exercise, adequate rest, and good nutrition. These are *your* responsibilities as a parent. What may seem like an aggressive behavior problem could actually be a physical problem related to blood-sugar levels. I'm amazed at the number of kids who have a cola and a doughnut for breakfast, french fries for lunch, no supper, but a milkshake later in the evening. Who wouldn't begin to experience problems from that kind of food?

Kids don't need to be in an organized sports program to get exercise. Encourage such healthy activities as walking, jogging, biking, tennis, swimming, to name a few. Do it *with* them. Model a playful spirit around them. Wrestle around on the floor with your teen. Take him to a driving range and let him hit a bucket of golf balls. Teens need some physical outlets for their aggression and stress.

Try to keep your teen interested in church or church-related activities. I've seen an active church youth group help keep marginal kids from going over the edge. At the same time, if the youth group is exclusive or "cliquish," nothing could be worse than forcing your teen to attend. So check out your church's youth group before you push too hard. It may be that it would be better to suggest involvement in a school-based group, such as Young Life, which tends to be more inclusive and less "churchy." The goal here is to put your teen in contact with other Christian kids to talk to as well as with caring leaders who will be there when they're needed.

It's a cruel, cruel world

High school kids can be almost sadistic in their treatment of each other. Insults become an art form, and the pack mentality can reduce a loner or someone who's different to devolve into an inner world of psychosis. One of the most disturbing things I hear from troubled kids is the way that they are treated by "the *in* crowd." In most schools those are the athletes, cheerleaders, and "social gadflies" who decide who's cool and who's not.

Please take time to warn your teens about the dangers of harassing other kids. Often they do not intend to be cruel and would never really want to drive someone to the point of suicide or psychotic behavior. They just don't know what could happen. Let them know, and if possible, arrange for them to visit a mental health facility. Once they see the outcome of peer abuse and ridicule, they may never participate again.

Ideally, you can convince your teen of the virtue in standing up for those who are victims of cruel abuse. That may not initially make them very popular, but in the long run they will be respected by their peers. All it usually takes for the teasing to stop is one brave guy or girl to stick up for a kid when he's being teased. If the right people stand up to be counted, it can even be "cool" to intervene.

Mental health issues are extremely complex—far beyond my ability to comprehend or explain in this brief space, but I have noticed an increase in the number of kids being treated for some form of mental illness. It is something that every parent must take seriously, and it is imperative that you never try to cover up such problems if they exist in your family. Take advantage of all the excellent resources available for you and your teen should it become necessary to seek treatment.

12

TWENTY PRESCRIPTIONS FOR EFFECTIVE COMMUNICATION WITH TEENAGERS

Are you communicating well with your teenager? You aren't alone if you feel that you're not getting through. In spite of all our advances in global communications in this information age, many parents do not know how to talk and listen to their own sons or daughters. You can dial-direct to Moscow, but you can't get through to the teen who sleeps in the bedroom just down the hall. Far too often the atmosphere in the average home is strained, and frequently it is downright turbulent. Instead of a haven of peace, the average family resembles a war zone.

After speaking to four million kids in person and personally counseling thousands of young people, I have reflected on what they have told me. I've *really* listened. The following "Twenty Prescriptions for Effective Com-

149

munication with Teenagers" will work. Give them a try today, and practice them for many tomorrows.

Prescription #1. *Start listening today.* It's not too late even if you have an older teen and you haven't done a very good job of communicating with each other. Some of your teen's efforts to "talk" to you will be nonverbal (a change in behavior, more scowling or glaring, or the like). Most of the time they will try to communicate with a quick passing comment that you might think is insignificant. If you focus more on listening than on talking, you will begin to hear more sensitively.

A mother recently wrote to me and shared how her daughter, Jenny, had committed suicide. Jenny was called "California Sunshine" at school and was known for her good attitude and scholastic determination. When Jenny learned that her boyfriend was getting married, something went terribly wrong. Her sister walked into her bedroom one day and found Jenny dying of a self-inflicted gunshot wound to her head.

"Like all parents, we took too much for granted," her mother wrote. "I swallowed her bright exterior." Too often parents aren't listening. They don't hear their teen's idle comments in the car, at the dinner table, or at home. And the kids know it.

Start listening to them today! Discern their attitude, their fears, their emotions, their hangups, by what they are saying.

Prescription #2. *Read the signals.* Teens are always sending out message signals, either directly or indirectly. As a teenager in the drug scene I sent out signals to my parents, but they didn't seem to notice or care. Almost every Friday night I came home stoned, but Dad and Mom never seemed to detect that I was trying to send them a message. Don't be too hard on my folks, though. This still happens frequently in homes today.

My dad later told me, "Jerry, the reason I didn't see the message signals was that I did not want to see them." That's normal. What parent wants to hear bad news about his teen? We do not want to believe that we have problems in our families. For Christians this attitude of denial is even more of a problem. "What will our friends at church say?" is a question that also keeps us from listening. But to ignore the signals is just another way of saying, "I don't care about you" to your son or daughter.

If you sense that there's a problem, show your love by saying, "Hey Teresa, what's up? Things okay?" Then listen. Don't pry or try to badger information out of your kids. Just show that you noticed the signal. If they don't talk now, they will later. They need to believe that you *really* care and aren't just trying to get the goods on them. Message signals can include the friends they are hanging out with, the books they read, the favorite songs they play repeatedly, the notes they write, the way they dress. Abrupt or drastic changes in any of these areas is a tip-off that something's wrong. Get your "sensor receptor" out and catch every signal.

Prescription #3. *Be discerning.* But don't be a detective and don't go on a witch-hunt. Look at what your son or daughter enjoys. Notice the friends your child hangs out with and get to know them. Observe your teens' interests and ask yourself, "Is this healthy? Is it going to help or hurt them?"

A discerning parent can spot a problem before tragedy occurs. If you sense that something is wrong, do something but don't overreact. You are not dealing with an enemy—you are trying to help a cherished loved one. Treat your son or daughter in the way that you would treat any friends if you suspected that they were in danger. In a very calm manner (maybe with a hug) say, "Let's talk. Let's get real."

151

If they start to open up, listen. Never reject them, no matter what your teens may say. It may be shocking. They may tell you that they have done something that you consider horrible. Hate the sin, love the sinner. If you berate them for telling you the truth, they will begin lying and telling you what you *want* to hear.

Believe me, your kids won't respect you if you fail to notice the obvious. You don't have to have a Ph.D. to notice things like alcohol- or drug use, a switch from Top 40 to heavy-metal, or a T-shirt emblazoned with a frightening image. So many kids have told me, "My parents are so dumb, I'm able to sneak my girlfriend up to their bedroom without them ever knowing it." I don't tell them that some parents notice it but are afraid to say anything.

Prescription #4. *Let your teen talk whenever about whatever.* When a teen is facing a problem or dilemma and something is happening within his or her heart and soul, that kid needs to talk. Generally it won't fit into your timetable. Your son or daughter may want to talk after a date. You will be tired, maybe even asleep already. If you beg off until morning, you are shutting down an avenue of communication that probably won't be there in the morning when *you* want to talk.

To open up those avenues, set a specific time with your kids when they can talk. Let them know that it's their exclusive time to open up—and let it rip on any subject. At first they may not have much to say, but once they see that you really want to listen they will talk your leg off. In addition to this prescribed, regular time, however, be willing to drop everything if your teen ever comes up to you and says, "I've got something important I'd like to talk to you about." When your teen wants to talk with you, make time to listen.

Prescription #5. *Show your love.* The strongest single communication tool that you can use with your son or daughter is *love*. Yet I can't believe how many kids have told me that their parents don't love them. I can't say enough about the imperative of love in a parent-teen relationship. Of course you love your teenagers. You just may not be displaying it enough. I know that it's hard to love someone who is becoming independent of you and may even treat you poorly. But perhaps more than any other age group, teens need to *know* that they are loved.

One way to make sure that your teens know that they are loved is to tell them. Tell them again and again and again. Write it on notes in their lunches; end phone calls from them with, "I love you"; hug them often; and whisper that you love them. Sure, they may act embarrassed or put off, but believe me, they thrive on those words. I know, because I've heard so many kids tell me that they wished their parents had told them that they loved them.

A tangible expression of love is time. If somebody asks me how a teen would spell the word "love" for his parents, it would be T-I-M-E. In fact, verbally expressing our love without backing it up in action can be confusing and depressing for teens. Take time to share their teens' hobbies, interests, and activities. If your son is in the school play, don't miss it. If your daughter is on the basketball team, try to attend as many games as you can. Surprise your teen by taking off from work early and picking him up after school for a soda. Anything you do together that takes time will show how much you love them.

I have also found that love is inseparably connected with respect. Don't call your kids names or curse at them, no matter how much they upset you. They will close their ears later when you try to tell you them you love them. If you do blow your temper (which will happen), humble yourself and apologize. Teens appreciate people who are real, and they will love you more when they hear you say, "I'm sorry."

I tell my three kids that I love them every day I am with them or talk to them on the phone. Jeremy, ten, has picked up on that and tells me every day that he loves me. But it started with me. Start this habit in your home.

Prescription #6. *Be a confidant to your teenager.* A confidant is one to whom secrets are given without fear. Most teens have had a friend betray them and long to have someone in whom they can really confide. Why couldn't that be you? It is so easy to make friends with a teenager. Every teen I know is looking for someone to befriend him, understand him—someone to talk to and share problems with.

When I speak in a high school, the kids don't know me outside of the introduction and my address. Yet, afterward they stream to the front of the auditorium to talk with me. I could stay in a high school all day after one of my presentations, because so many want to talk. Simply through my story and the anecdotes I use, they perceive that I will listen. They're also pretty certain that I won't violate their trust. So they really open up.

Let your children know that they can tell you anything. *Anything!* Then be prepared when they drop the bomb. They might tell you some things that will shock you: "I've been getting drunk every Friday night." "I think I'm pregnant." "I don't believe in God anymore." Let them talk. Bite your lip and stifle the urge to set them straight. Be a confidant.

Prescription #7. *Don't be a nagger.* Many parents have eliminated any opportunity for communication because they have become a super critic of their teenager. One girl said to me, "My mom and dad don't know anything that is right with me. Mom is a college graduate who is working on more courses. Every time I go home, she always finds something wrong with me." How tragic, especially when you hear the rest of her story. At night she walks the streets as a prostitute without anyone's knowing that she works the streets. If a teen is rejected by his parents, he will try to find acceptance elsewhere, usually where we don't approve.

Don't nag. Don't notice every failure, every slip-up. When you point out a problem, do it in a straightforward, dispassionate manner. Don't start off with "You never," or "You always." Kids make mistakes and they know that they do. You don't need to itemize every one of them.

Prescription #8. *Emphasize the good.* Look for two specific attributes, talents, or abilities in your son or daughter and continually praise them. This is so important! Kids do many things wrong. After all, they're just kids. Nevertheless, every teen has plenty of talent and ability. Watch for the good things that your teen does, then reward him or her with a heartfelt word of praise. Not only will your teen benefit, but you will, too. Praising a child feels so much better than picking on him.

Prescription #9. *Model proper respect for authority.* Impress upon your teenager that you will always support the authorities in his or her life but that you will also see that he or she is treated fairly and equally. It does no good for your teenager for you to tear down a school teacher, law enforcement official, preacher, or whoever is in a position of authority. When you do that, in essence you are chipping away at your own authority over your child.

This is why it is so crucial not to get cross-grained with teachers, coaches, and ministers. Kids take their cues from parents. Back those individuals who work with your child. Show respect for the law in the little things you do: safe driving, wearing seat belts, avoiding littering, telling the clerk when you've been *undercharged.*

America incarcerates more people than does any nation on earth. Our prisons are overcrowded with a projected 1.5 million persons behind bars by the year 2000 A.D. Some of these prisoners learned from their parents to question, challenge, and reject authority over them.

Prescription #10. *Demand the best but not perfection.* When you are tempted to scold your teen for having gotten a B instead of an A, try to visualize the faces of the kids who have committed suicide because of too-high parental expectations. Their moms and dads were not content for a son or daughter to simply do his best. They wanted their child to be Number One, to wear the brass ring. So the child quietly exited this world. One university student found dead left this note: "I tried to live up to your expectations all those years and I finally realized I can't."

Not everyone is going to have a 4.0 GPA or be a star on the varsity basketball team. Some kids are destined to sit on the bench no matter how hard they try. Others will get cut from the play or music group at school. Make sure that your teens know that they can fail. Focus on effort more than on performance. And if they work hard to make the team but still get cut, be there with an encouraging word.

Prescription #11. *Be generous with hugs.* Everyone loves to be hugged, but I've observed that parents quit hugging their kids at about age twelve. A BIG mistake. There's something about physical attention and a teenager that says, "Mom and Dad really care about me."

How long *has* it been since you hugged your teenage son or daughter? How long has it been since you reached out to caress a hand or give a tender pat on the head? Do they know that they are more important than your car, your hobbies, your new gadget, or your friends?

Sometimes when things are going poorly between you and your teens, the best thing that you can do is to go up to them and without saying a word give them a big hug and hold onto them for a few seconds. Deep down inside they long for that kind of physical evidence of your love. Maybe you do, too.

Prescription #12. *Know what to overlook.* Teens will make some big blunders. Sometimes they will repeat the same mistakes. Let those mistakes remind you that they are human, not perfect. Don't point out every error. Choose your "battles" wisely. Take everything in balance. Do you really need to tell your child every night that her room is a mess and that she needs to do a better job of cleaning it? Is his hairstyle *that* important?

I'm amazed at the number of parents who make a big thing about such matters as not hanging up the towel after a shower but then ignore needle marks on their teen's arms. Whenever you find yourself ready to get after your teen about something, ask yourself, "What will I gain from pointing out this mistake?" Then opt for mercy.

Prescription #13. *Allow your teenager some privacy.* Don't force your teen to talk when she doesn't want to. Eventually she'll open up, especially if you've been working on creating an atmosphere of trust. Kids have repeatedly complained to me: "My parents are on top of me all the time. I can't handle that anymore."

Some parents go overboard. Instead of being discerning, they become Sherlock Holmes. They are constantly jumping to some evil-inspired conclusion about their teen. They are certain that their teen is up to no good, and to prove it they go around with a spyglass just looking for trouble.

Relax, or as kids sometimes say, "Chill out!" Give your child (and yourself) some breathing room. Make sure that they have some private time at home and a place where they can be alone. Leave the room when they talk on the phone. Don't go snooping in their dresser or closet. Give kids their privacy, and they will be more likely to open up to you on the things that really count.

Prescription #14. *Notice your teen's friends.* You can't choose your teen's friends for her, but you can notice them. Insist that you be introduced, and please show an interest in them. If possible, have them over. It's harder to make poor choices of friends if one knows that one's parents will be talking to them, having them over, taking an active role in knowing them. Besides, kids are neat—you'll enjoy it!

At times, a teen will go with the flow, not really wanting to do what is wrong but unable to speak up. So the type of kid that your teen hangs out with is very important. If you sense that your teen is under pressure from his friends—if he seems too eager to go with them every time they drop by or call—intervene in love. Give him advice. Allow him to use you as an excuse to say no ("I can't tonight, my parents won't let me").

When I got into drugs, I was pressured by what I thought was a friend. Rob just wouldn't give up. Only three hours after meeting me at school on that first day, he offered me a joint. I didn't want to get high. I told him that. But I was afraid of losing him as a friend. I stayed away from him for three days, spending more time than ever in my home with my parents and brothers. I wanted so badly to tell them that this kid was trying to turn me on to drugs, but I just couldn't. If only I could have. I ended up getting heavily involved in the drug scene.

Now Rob was one truly messed-up kid. Both parents were alcoholics and his older brother was a speed freak. Everyone knew it, but my parents never monitored my friends. If they had watched and observed, they would have noticed that Rob wasn't a good choice for me.

Monitor your teen's choice of friends and don't be afraid to intervene.

Prescription #15. *Control your anger.* Teens are at an age where they will naturally challenge their parents and won't always be tactful or civil in their rebellion. In short, they know exactly how to light your fuse! You *will* get angry from time to time, and that's fine. Just stay in control.

Once you start screaming, your teen will have conquered you. You will realize that and scream even louder. What might have been a slight disagreement has now become a fight. In the end, you will be the loser in your eyes and in the eyes of your teen. Nothing will have been gained, and the communication gap will have become wider.

So many times I hear kids tell me, "All my dad does is yell at me." If it helps, use the "count to ten" rule before you respond to something your child has done. Or if you are especially angry, be honest with your teen: "I am so mad I really don't think we should talk about it until I cool down, so go to your room for a while." Those words delivered in a cool, controlled tone can have a more desirable effect than shouting your criticism.

Keep in mind that if you blow up over every little thing, your teen will soon tune you out. A teenager is an expert at blanking out during a parent's diatribe. But that's not communication.

Prescription #16. *Be your teen's best role model.* Many young people say to me, "Jerry, my parents tell me not to smoke pot or get drunk, while they get bombed with their friends every Saturday night." Or "I don't do drugs, my parents do," is another frequent comment. How can you honestly expect your child to do something that *you* aren't willing to do?

When a parent figuratively says, "Do as I say, not as I do," kids walk away feeling that their parents are hypocrites. A teenager will identify quicker with an imperfect but honest parent than with one who only works at an image of perfection. If you have a drinking problem, admit it to your teen. Believe me, they already know, but they will be magnetized to a parent who is willing to make such an admission. Also, you are modeling what you want them to do if they have a problem.

Being a good role model does not mean being a perfect person. In fact, some of the most effective parents I have met are ones who are working to overcome major hangups in their lives.

Prescription #17. *Be honest with your discipline.* Every teenager needs the security of having a parent who cares enough to do something about disobedience and harmful behavior. We are not doing a favor to a son or daughter when we do not discipline them.

At an elite private academy, fifteen-year-old Aaron told me, "My father has given me everything—a motorcycle, boat, car. I don't want all that as much as I want my dad. I want to know that he really cares about the way I am and how messed up my life is." Aaron had almost never been disciplined.

Being honest with your discipline means carrying through on your threats, making the punishment fit the crime, disciplining in love rather than anger. Proper, controlled discipline breeds a deep security within the life of any child. It assures him that his parents still care.

I also think that it's important to admit it when you've made a mistake in discipline, especially if you've made an unreasonable threat in a moment of anger. Instead of just ignoring the threat, go to your teen and explain that you were upset, and that you realize that the punishment is too severe for the infraction. But then explain the new punishment. This will communicate volumes to your teen about honesty and love. She will take her medicine more easily when she sees you adjust the dosage.

Prescription #18. *Seek a few valuable allies.* Every teen has at least one other adult that he or she looks up to. Some have many. Beyond the movie stars, athletic heroes, and musicians, there is a special teacher, coach, or neighbor who is held in high esteem. Form an alliance with that special individual who has rapport with your teen. Don't try to exploit that relationship or use it to dig up dirt about your teen. Just let that person know that you are glad that she is in a position of influence over your teen and that you want to support her.

If you come to a point where you feel your rapport is gone with your teen, go to that person and explain your concern. Be honest and tell the whole story. Then ask this ally to help tear down the wall that has gone up between you and your teen. This takes great humility and can be somewhat awkward for everyone, but in the long run it can help you during those rough times that every parent will have with a teenager.

Prescription #19. *Pray with your teen.* I have found that if I really want to get to know someone—how they think, what really concerns them—all I have to do is regularly pray with them. Praying with a teen is better than talking!

If you do not pray regularly with your teen, start today. Explain that you want to correct an oversight, that you believe that prayer really helps, and that you want to pray together every day. Don't put your kid on the spot and make him pray out loud at first. Simply utter a prayer for your teen's safety and well-being and for you as a parent. Eventually invite her to join with a prayer of her own. Do this before school or at night just before bedtime and try to make it a habit. It will build a strong bond between you that normal conversation cannot.

One other thing I've noticed. It's hard to stay mad at someone whom you pray with.

Prescription #20. *Plan at least one special event with your teen each month.* This activity should involve just you and your teen. Don't bring your spouse; don't let your teen bring a friend. Go it alone. There are thousands of things that you can do alone with your teen. Go for a walk in the park. Stop for a soda. Build a bird feeder together. Go fishing. See a new movie. Watch the stars. Climb a tree. Explore a bookstore. Sit on a bench at the mall. Fly a kite. The activity isn't as important as the time alone you will have with your teen.

I know that you are busy. So am I. I've logged nearly a million miles on one airline alone. My work is important, but so are my kids. Their greatest excitement comes when we plan something together. Remember that in just a few very brief years—they will be gone. As much as you will want to spend some regular, quality time with them, you won't be able to. So do it *now.* Set aside the other stuff and make this effort. When you pull out of the driveway alone with your teen, she will know she is important to you.

Wouldn't it be great if your teen thought of you or your spouse as a best friend? It can happen.

A special word from Jerry:

You can't incorporate all of these prescriptions into your life at one time. Pick five to try today, this week. *Work* at them. Make them as natural as breathing. Then pick five more. Within a few months you will have made all twenty a vital aspect of your relationship with your teen. You will have become an effective communicator with that lovable but difficult young person. May God bless your efforts!

13

KIDS ON THE EDGE: WARNING SIGNALS

Some parents are tragically inattentive to problems festering in their teenager's life. Robbie, living in a rural area, told me how his dad regularly called the sheriff's department to check on drug use in the area. Robbie was a user. His dad hadn't even noticed.

Teens do exhibit warning signals when things are going wrong. The following "Kids on the Edge: Warning Signals" could indicate drug or alcohol abuse, suicidal tendencies, occult activity, or one of many other teen problems needing careful attention. If you notice any of these signals in your teen, serious difficulties may be ahead if you don't begin to intervene with love and care.

1. Dramatic, noticeable change in personality
   - loss of interest in former activities
   - marked difference in disposition
   - sudden mood changes

2. Change in educational or academic progress
   - skipping classes
   - a sudden drop in grades
   - repeated behavior problems with faculty or peers

3. Aggressive, violent behavior at home
   - concealing a firearm, knife, or other weapon
   - signs of self-mutilation or tattoos
   - experimenting with fire or homemade explosives

4. Odd, unexplainable change in friends
   - reluctance to bring friends home
   - little or no contact with former friends

5. Withdrawal from family, friends, and former activities
   - mysterious isolation
   - total disinterest in previous hobbies and interests
   - unusually quiet

6. Dramatic physical changes
   - sudden weight gain or loss
   - new sloppiness or neatness
   - distinct new aroma

7. Unexplained need for money
   - stealing or borrowing excessive amounts
   - going through money with little to show for it

Young people who exhibit one or more of these signs are reaching out for help. Be there for them. Sometimes regular counseling is needed. Occasionally, hospitalization or residency at an adolescent recovery unit may be necessary. Don't wait until it's too late.

Finally, don't go it alone. When serious problems arise with teens, I recommend a team approach involving church (pastor, youth pastor), school (counselor, social worker, teacher, coach), and community (medical and psychological clinics, social service agencies, law enforcement agencies). Persons in these resources have a professional and personal interest in helping people.

Epilogue

The only thing necessary for the triumph of evil is for good men [and women] to do nothing.

—Edmund Burke

Throughout *Who's Listening?* I have enumerated and defined the nature of the major spiritual ills afflicting young persons today. Hundreds of thousands of teenage children in our "great" American society are, literally, the walking wounded. They're disillusioned, scandalized, and demoralized at a period in their lives that should be uniquely graced with love and security and hope for the future. Too often the victims of parental and societal neglect, they're the target of insidiously orchestrated pressures to ignore the Ten Commandments, then they're abandoned to suffer the inevitable consequences of their vulnerability.

It is simply not enough just to be appalled by the grim statistics underscored in this book: Concerned adults who *really* want to preserve America's most endangered species—its young people—must ACT in various ways to reverse the tidal wave of disaffection, alienation, and moral corruption that is drowning our most precious commodity: our teenage children.

What, actually, *can* one person do to rekindle the quenched fires of hope and trust and emotional well-being among our teenage, old-before-their-time kids? Although there is no quick fix, there *are* positive actions that can be taken to slowly but surely restore spiritual, mental, and emotional strength to these fragile future adults: As a beginning, re-read and take to heart the twenty prescriptions for effective communication with teenagers in chapter 12. They bear repeating:

1. *Start listening today* to your teenager.
2. *Read the signals* that your teenager is wigwagging at you.
3. *Be discerning* and approachable.
4. *Let your teen talk whenever and about whatever* even if it doesn't fit into your timetable.
5. *Show your love,* unconditionally.
6. *Be a confidant to your teenager,* a befriender.
7. *Don't be a nagger* ("Fathers [mothers], do not exasperate your children; instead, bring them up in the training and instruction of the Lord" [Ephesians 6:4]).
8. Extremely important: *Emphasize the good* that your teenager displays.
9. Model proper respect for authority.
10. *Demand the best but not perfection,* focusing more on effort than on performance.
11. *Be generous with hugs.*
12. *Know what to overlook,* remembering that your teen is human and can make mistakes.
13. *Allow your teenager some privacy.*
14. *Take an interest in your teen's friends.*
15. Above all, *control your anger.*
16. *Be your teen's best role model.*
17. Because you do not do a favor to a son or daughter if you are afraid to discipline, *be honest with your*

discipline, making the punishment fit the "crime" and disciplining in love, not anger.

18. *Form an alliance with any special individual who has rapport with your teen* (you need all the help you can get).

19. Most powerful of all remedial actions, *pray* with your teen—*regularly*, explaining that you believe in the power of prayer for your mutual well-being and safety.

20. Last, and more important than it may seem at face value, *plan at least one special event each month involving only you and your teen* to explore and renew all the beautiful things that you have forgotten that you have in common.

Other options/remedies/challenges

Provide comfortable alternatives such as allowing your kids to bring other kids home with them to share community and camaraderie. Or propose to your church that a room (it doesn't have to be fancy) be set aside as a refuge from the hurly-burly of life, where kids can gather for fellowship and moral support. *Convince* the kids who frequent your home and/or the church youth center that in you they have a friend—someone who cares about their problems and who will listen if they want to talk to someone they can trust.

Challenge churches to set priorities—who or what is more important than our kids? Pool the talents of various individuals in your church to offer their time and their compassion to befriend teenagers who need to tap the wells of their wisdom and experience. Don't leave Big Brother-ing and Big Sister-ing up to community social services—get involved with the nurturing of *any* kid (not just your own) who needs help!

Challenge local, state, and federal government to get tougher on pornographers, drug suppliers, and pushers, sexual offenders (especially child molesters), and to exact tougher punishment for the murder of the hearts and minds of our kids—laws severe enough to deter criminal activities against our youth. Become a burr under the saddles of political, legal, medical, and social service professions.

Join or form neighborhood watches that will not just be on the lookout for human predators of our kids but who will be *spiritual* paramedics who are available for all emergencies. Establish in your community a twenty-four-hour 9-1-1–K-I-D-S hotline for troubled teens, a hotline that will not only listen but will *unconditionally* follow up in love.

Offer closer cooperation with the law enforcement agencies in your community, who are always grateful for grass roots citizen support. *Form a Concerned Parent-Citizen committee in your community* to disclose the identity of would-be molesters, pornographers, drug dealers, and all other corrupters of youth who rely on the passivity and indifference of society toward them to stay in "business."

Child preservers should take a cue from Senator William Proxmire's watchdog surveillance for outstanding violations of common sense and integrity: the "Golden Fleece" award, given for breaches of public trust. *Why not create a monthly or semi-annual Millstone Award* (to be bestowed with much publicity) upon the outstanding scandalizers of children and providers of toxic waste entertainment in television, movies, magazines, and radio programs? (The name of the Millstone Award would derive from Mark 9:42: "And whosoever shall scandalize one of these little ones that believe in me; it were better for him that a millstone were hanged about his neck, and he were cast into the sea.")

Inspire an ongoing letter-writing campaign, not just to congresspersons on the state and federal level but to government agencies, law enforcement agencies, social service departments, and to local, state, and federal legal associations, mental health agencies, education associations, and medical societies—enlisting their help. Especially ameliorative might be ongoing letter-writing campaigns to those companies and businesses that endorse suggestive, coarse, sexually explicit, or vulgar messages by their sponsorship of certain programs or commercials. (It has been determined that these sponsors are sensitive to sincere criticism and will withdraw their sponsorship if shown that consumers will boycott their product if they do not.)

The foregoing are only a few of the many possible, effective means by which concerned parents and cherishers of youth can change the present descent into dehumanization of the young. If enough good men and women put their heads together and unite their creative efforts, we can reclaim our moral obligation and authority to shield and protect our kids from everything that is harmful to their health—spiritually, mentally, and physically!

And, more consequential than any of the preceding calls-to-arms, is our option to *love* each and every young person who is crying out to parents and adults for attention and *positive* role models. Good parents and mentors have it in their power to affect eternity by their moral support and defense of the young. This is not oversimplification: In unity there *is* strength. By our caring, we can love hurt and hurting kids into the kingdom.

Resources to Help You

If you or someone you know needs additional help in the areas discussed in this book, the following resources are good places to start:

Abortion

The following toll-free numbers will put you in touch with people whose goal is to counsel young women into keeping their babies:

1-800-848-LOVE
1-800-BETHANY
1-800-A FAMILY

For literature, write or phone:

National Right to Life (NRL) Trust Fund
419 7th Street N.W., Suite 500
Washington, D.C. 20004
(202) 626-8809

Alcohol

These organizations have a vital interest in keeping kids free from alcohol use:

(508) 481-3568 (Students Against Driving Drunk)
(214) 744-6233 (Mothers Against Drunk Driving)
(518) 362-9624 (Remove Intoxicated Drivers)

Also, consult your Yellow Pages under Alcoholism Information and Treatment Centers. Most local hospitals have programs for teens who are heavy alcohol users, or they can refer you to such clinics.

For literature, write or phone:

Al-Anon World Service Headquarters, Inc.
1372 Broadway
New York, NY 10018
(212) 302-7240

Alateen
P.O. Box 182
New York, NY 10159-0182
(212) 254-7230

AIDS

(800) 342-2437 Hotline—Center for Disease Control
(800) 458-5231 Information Line
(404) 332-4555 Health Information—Center for
    Disease Control
(404) 488-5323 Health Education—Center for
    Disease Control

For literature write or phone:

Center for Disease Control
Office of Public Affairs
1600 Clifton Road, N.E.
Bldg. 1, Rm. 2067, Mailstop D-25
Atlanta, GA 30333

National AIDS Clearinghouse
P.O. Box 6003
Rockville, MD 20849-6003

Drugs

(800) 782-3327 Cedar Ridge Treatment Facility
(800) NCA-CALL National Council on
    Alcoholism/Drug Dependence

In your Yellow Pages see Drug Abuse and Addiction—Information and Treatment.

Family Problems

(800) 422-4453 Child Help/Parents Anonymous

In your Yellow Pages see Marriage and Family Counseling.

For literature write or phone:

CHILDHELP
6733 S. Sepulveda
Los Angeles, CA 90046
(800) 422-4453

When parenting is getting the best of you or you are in a crisis situation, this organization will get you help immediately or refer you to someone who can.

FAMILY RESOURCE COALITION
236 N. Michigan Ave., Suite 1625
Chicago, IL 60601
(312) 341-0900

A clearinghouse for family resource programs throughout the United States and Canada.

Physical / Sexual Abuse

(800) 422-4453

In your Yellow Pages see Crisis Intervention Services.

For literature write or phone:

CHILDHELP
P.O. Box 630
Hollywood, CA 90028

National Center on Child Abuse/Neglect
P.O. Box 1182
Washington, DC 20013
(301) 251-5157

Violence

(800) 638-8736 Juvenile Justice Clearinghouse
(800) 732-3277 Bureau of Justice Statistics
(800) 627-6872 National Criminal Justice Reference
Service—information and publications

In your Yellow Pages see your local Crisis Intervention
Center and/or your local police department.

Mental Health

(800) SVA-TEEN (782-8336) JERRY JOHNSTON'S HOT-
LINE—answered by trained professionals of Century Health
Care Corp., the national leader in adolescent mental and emo-
tional recovery.

Minirth-Meier Clinic
P.O. Box 1925
Richardson, TX 75085
(800) 228-3000

Satanism and the Occult

(312) 267-7777 Cult Awareness Network

For information or literature write:

Cult Awareness Network
2421 W. Pratt Boulevard, Suite 1173
Chicago, IL 60645

The Cult Awareness Network is an organization that
monitors destructive cult activity.

American Family Foundation
P.O. Box 2265
Bonita Springs, FL 33959-2265
(212) 249-7693

Other sources for help or information:

(800) 999-9999 Covenant House—A national directory
of hotlines
(918) 258-9651 Century Health Care, recommended by
Jerry Johnston